MOMMY, I CAN'T BREATHE

The Modern Guide to Navigate
Allergies and Asthma

Reneé Matthews, M.D.

Chicago and Detroit

Copyright © 2021 Reneé Matthews, M.D.
First edition
Sterling Walton Press
Chicago, IL, and Detroit, MI

All rights reserved. No portion of this book may be reproduced or transmitted in any form or by means, electronic or mechanical, including photocopying, recording, or by any information storage or retrieval system, without the written consent of the publisher. Contact Sterling Walton Press for inquiries and media at inquires@askdrrenee.info.

ISBN: 978-1-7368358-1-4

Cover design by Eva Wilson
Interior Layout: Kimolisa Mings

I dedicate this book to
my loving mother, Rev. Joyce Matthews.
She always makes sure I can breathe,
which is why I could write this book.

Contents

INTRODUCTION 1

MY LIFE STORY 4
    THE BIRTH 4
    RENEE'S REMEDY 8

MOMMY'S HELPER 9
    RENEE'S REMEDY 10

FAMILY TIMES 11

GOING TO SCHOOL 15
    RENEE'S REMEDY 19

GIRL SCOUT CAMP 20
    RENEE'S REMEDY 21

FIFTH GRADE HOSPITALIZATION 22
    RENEE'S REMEDY 23

URGENT CARE EXPERIENCE 24
    RENEE'S REMEDY 25

THE FUNERAL 26
    RENEE'S REMEDY 27

OLIVER! 28
    RENEE'S REMEDY 29

BABYSITTING 30
    RENEE'S REMEDY 31

PAPER ROUTE 32
    RENEE'S REMEDY 32
MY DANCING DAYS 33
    RENEE'S REMEDY 34
SLEEPOVER CAMP 35
    RENEE'S REMEDY 36
HIGH SCHOOL 37
    RENEE'S REMEDY 38
COLLEGE DAYS 40
    RENEE'S REMEDY 41
I CAN'T BREATHE 42
    RENEE'S REMEDY 43
BANANA MUFFINS 44
    RENEE'S REMEDY 45
CLASS OF 1999 46
    RENEE'S REMEDY 46
DAD'S COOKING 48
    RENEE'S REMEDY 49
ASTHMA STUDIES 50
    RENEE'S REMEDY 50
SEAFOOD RESTAURANT OUTING 51
    RENEE'S REMEDY 52
BUYING EGGS 53
    RENEE'S REMEDY 53
ACCIDENTAL EPIPEN 55
    RENEE'S REMEDY 55

IS CHICKEN CURRY EQUAL TO CURRY CHICKEN? 56
    RENEE'S REMEDY 57
LUNCH WITH MY MENTOR 58
    RENEE'S REMEDY 58
ICE SCREAM YOU SCREAM 60
    RENEE'S REMEDY 61
DESSERT ANYONE? 62
    RENEE'S REMEDY 62
FOOD ALLERGY EXPO 63
    RENEE'S REMEDY 64
HALF MARATHON 65
    RENEE'S REMEDY 66
SAVED BY R&B CROONER 68
    RENEE'S REMEDY 69
INFLUENCER PERKS 70
    RENEE'S REMEDY 71
CHICAGO FONDUE RESTAURANT 72
    RENEE'S REMEDY 72
SISTER'S TRIP 73
    RENEE'S REMEDY 74
ESSENCE FEST NUTS AT RESTAURANT 75
    RENEE'S REMEDY 76
GETTING RID OF NEGATIVITY 77
Prologue 79
WHAT IS ASTHMA? 81
    DEFINITION OF ASTHMA 81
    ASTHMA ATTACK 82

    ORIGIN AND CAUSE 82
    DOCTORS DIAGNOSE ASTHMA 84
    TREATMENT 85
    MONITORING 86
ASTHMA STATISTICS 88
ASTHMA IN CHILDREN 89
    WHAT ARE THE SIGNS AND SYMPTOMS? 89
    HIDDEN ASTHMA 89
    WHAT USUALLY TRIGGERS ASTHMA? 90
RISK FACTORS FOR DEVELOPING ASTHMA 93
    RISK FACTORS FOR ASTHMA 93
    What Can Be Done 97
TYPES AND CAUSES OF ASTHMA 99
    New Classifications In Types Of Asthma 100
EXERCISE-INDUCED ASTHMA 103
NOCTURNAL ASTHMA 107
OCCUPATIONAL ASTHMA 113
HOW TO TELL IF YOU HAVE ASTHMA 118
HOW YOUR DOCTOR DIAGNOSES ASTHMA 121
WHAT DOES A PULMONOLOGIST DO? 126
SHOULD I SEE AN ALLERGIST? 133
ALLERGY TESTING FOR CHILDREN 137
TIPS FOR CONTROLLING YOUR ASTHMA 141
ASTHMA ATTACKS 145
HOW IS ASTHMA TREATED 148
UNDERSTANDING THE DIFFERENT TYPES OF ASTHMA

MEDICATIONS 152
ALLERGY OVERVIEW 159
ASTHMA AND ECZEMA.. 170
OSTEOPOROSIS 174
LIVING WITH ASTHMA... 182
RECOGNIZING ASTHMA SYMPTOMS AND TRIGGERS ... 185
AIR POLLUTION AND OUTDOOR TRIGGERS...................... 189
CONTROLLING ASTHMA TRIGGERS IN THE HOME......... 192
THE BACK-TO-SCHOOL SEASON AND ASTHMA................ 195
MANAGING ASTHMA IN THE SCHOOL ENVIRONMENT
.... 198
TRAVELING WITH ASTHMA 206
METERED DOSE INHALER & HAND HELD NEBULIZER 209
BEST PRACTICES FOR EATING OUT 219
DR. RENEE'S RESTAURANTS 220
COMMON ALLERGENS 222
ABOUT THE AUTHOR 223
ACKNOWLEDGMENTS... 225
REFERENCES 227
INDEX 229

INTRODUCTION

"Mommy, I Can't Breathe" is a phrase my parents know too well. Ever since I was old enough to walk and talk, I used this phrase to wake them up. You see, asthma attacks usually happen at night. I will explain later why this occurs.

Until I was ten years old and in the fifth grade, I went to the emergency room every night of October and April, complaining of a severe asthma attack. You had to understand that for me to go to the hospital meant that my breathing was seriously compromised. My mom is a respiratory therapist and was the director of a couple of respiratory departments at Level 1 trauma centers while I was growing up. Did I mention that she taught respiratory therapy to a whole generation of therapists in the Detroit area before taking those jobs? There were not many hospitals where she didn't know at least one of the therapists. My mom also made sure I had all the equipment I needed to keep me alive. My allergist, Dr. Marva Morris, understood my mom was "in the business." Dr. Morris gave my mom her home number because sometimes when I was ready to go home from the emergency room, they wanted to keep me longer. Dr. Morris would explain to them that my mom knew best and that I was ready to go home.

Now, before we get too much further, I don't want you to think that I had this horrible childhood and missed so much school and other activities because of the severity of my asthma and food allergies. It was quite the opposite. My childhood was fantastic, and I think all kids are different and unique. One of my unique traits was severe asthma, and I was allergic to everything. Well, at least that is what everyone always seemed to say when I revealed my allergy list. Nevertheless, my parents took us on domestic and international trips, and I never landed in the hospital during these trips

I am writing this book so that you, as parents, guardians, and caregivers of someone with asthma or allergies, understand that life is enjoyable despite allergies and asthma. Also, I know many people are diagnosed with asthma and/or food allergies in adulthood. Hopefully, you can learn a thing or two to help ease your anxiety when you get the new diagnosis. You will learn how my mom navigated elementary school, how I navigated middle school, high school, college, medical school, and adulthood, how I have lived in two countries outside the United States, and how I have traveled to many more.

The book aims to help parents of children who struggle with allergies and asthma. I decided to write this book because I have lived my entire life with both. I don't remember not dealing with this challenging duo of allergies and asthma. Food allergies are now common, and as lots of people have asthma, I felt it was time to pen a book to help you traverse this complex and complicated—though manageable— world the way that I have.

In childhood asthma, the lungs and airways become easily inflamed when exposed to specific triggers, such as inhaling pollen or catching a cold or other respiratory infections. Childhood asthma can cause bothersome daily symptoms that interfere with play, sports, school, and sleep. In some children, unmanaged asthma can cause dangerous asthma attacks. Childhood asthma isn't a different disease from adult asthma, but children face unique challenges. The condition is a leading cause of emergency department visits, hospitalizations, and missed school days.

Unfortunately, you can't cure childhood asthma, and symptoms can continue into adulthood. But with the proper treatment, you and your child can keep symptoms under control and prevent damage to growing lungs.

MY LIFE STORY

THE BIRTH

My mom graduated from the University of Michigan with a Master of Science degree. She often wore house slippers because her feet were so swollen from pregnancy, and she couldn't fit in regular shoes. The day after her baby shower, she woke up early in the morning, around 6 a.m., to be precise. She was feeling so uncomfortable due to labor pains. She called the doctor and informed him that she would meet him at the hospital. My dad was heading to work that morning but was instructed by the doctor to accompany mom to the hospital. Hence, he had to sacrifice that morning's work for the family's responsibility.

I was born on August 30, 1976. with the umbilical cord wrapped around my neck. My Apgar score, a test given to newborns to evaluate their health against infant mortality, was a few points off because I didn't cry, and I was placed in an isolette (a clear plastic enclosed crib that isolates the infants from germs and provides oxygen) immediately. My arrival into this world was the beginning of something that I'd struggle with most of my life, which is a hard time breathing.

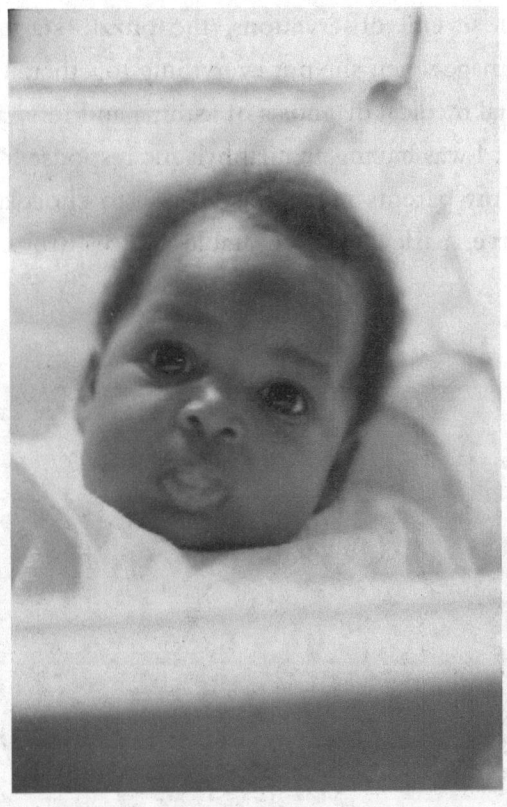

My mom wasn't too surprised about my condition since she was a respiratory therapist and an asthma survivor herself. My mom was given three-months maternity leave so she would be able to breastfeed. This is what she committed to do. At six months old, my parents started feeding me oatmeal to give me cereal plus breast milk, and it didn't take long before my mother realized this caused me to throw up on her every day. As a result, I stopped being fed formula since many kinds were not palatable with my system, so my mother put me back on milk. She used different types such as goat's milk, soy milk, and then Cremora. Yes, cream for coffee and nonfat dry milk. I was first fed a liquid formula with the goat's milk, and then I was given a powdered formula that could be mixed with water. My soy milk was a powdered formula as well. Based upon her knowledge and experiences, my mom quickly figured out that I was allergic to oatmeal. After several observations, the puzzle started to show a more precise image when she put everything together. This was when I had my official medical diagnosis of asthma and food allergies. They discovered that I was having an anaphylactic response to oatmeal.

They told my parents that I was allergic to chocolate, nuts, fish, eggs, wheat, rye, barley, raw vegetables, citrus fruits, cheese, and cow's milk.

When my mom went back to work after her leave, my Aunt Mary Walton, Auntie Mary as we affectionately called her, was my babysitter. Auntie Mary was the best because she understood me. I remember her restocking the house with what I could eat. She always served us what my mom suggested, including Cream of Rice. This was the only hot cereal I ate for a very long time since oatmeal was no longer an option due to my allergies. Cream of Wheat was not an option either. Most people are unfamiliar with Cream of Rice, but it is made by the same company that makes Cream of Wheat. The product is gluten-free and continues to gain popularity.

The Pediatrician found it so difficult to believe that I was having an asthma attack at two months of age, that he requested that my mother put the phone near me for the doctor to confirm and hear the high-pitched, coarse whistling sound that came from my tiny and weak body.

At two and a half years old, I started nursery school. It was a significant period because I became a big sister. My little sister Alycia, one of my primary taste testers when my parents were not around, was, on a few occasions, my lifesaver, but you will find out about those later. The preschool received this fabulous chart to explain what I could and could not eat. At preschool, I ate at least two meals a day and snacks. As soon as I could talk, I would ask my mom if I could eat whatever was around, and she would say, "No, you are allergic." It's how I learned of my allergies. Over time, I committed the list to memory, and at a very young age, I knew all my allergy triggers. I had an allergist by the time I was five years old.

RENEE'S REMEDY

Please pay attention to anything that seems out of the ordinary with your baby. If you have a family history of asthma and your baby's breathing sounds labored, take note of it and call the doctor. Once you have done so and the diagnosis is determined, take your child to the right specialist. You can see a pulmonologist for your asthma diagnosis. Also, an allergy and immunology physician can treat asthma and/or allergies as well. If your child has any reaction thought to be from food or something environmental, make sure an allergist does an allergy test to confirm what allergies are present to avoid triggers and help you both.

MOMMY'S HELPER

My sister, Alycia, is two and a half years my junior. When she was a baby, and I was roughly approaching three years old, our dad shopped for groceries while our mom was home with us. I was considered "mommy's little helper." I loved to help people, and so I was assisting my mom in putting groceries away.

Unfortunately, when I grabbed the eggs, that encounter didn't go well, and I ended up breaking one in my hands then rubbing it on my face.

Since she was tending to my sister, she didn't realize I had broken an egg until it was too late. "Oh, my goodness!" She cleaned me up, and the next day I got sick. During that hospital encounter, the doctor asked if she knew what triggered the attack. She couldn't figure out what could have caused the attack immediately until she remembered the broken egg all over me.

The event was a complete example of a delayed reaction. It was one of the many examples where I had an asthma attack because of my egg allergy. However, I didn't even eat the egg. Just the fact that the egg white and egg yolk came in contact with my face, mouth and eyes was enough to trigger the allergy.

I'm an adult now and a baker at heart. Guess what? I use eggs. I love baking and I crack the eggs open. How do I avoid an allergic reaction? I wash my hands immediately and throw the shells away. It is what I've learned to do to combat the problem, and it has worked.

RENEE'S REMEDY

This was the lesson in a delayed reaction. Just because you ate something you were allergic to twenty-four hours ago, keep in mind that you could still react. You may not be out of the woods just yet, so make no assumptions. Pay close attention to your body. You must seek treatment immediately if you are having breathing difficulties following any incidents that might trigger a reaction

FAMILY TIMES

Anytime my parents went out on the weekends or when school was out for a break, Auntie Mary took care of us. She had three teenagers living at home at the time, and they were very well versed in my allergies and always made sure I avoided things that triggered the allergy. And they also knew how to handle asthma emergencies.

My maternal grandmother had seven kids and was very active, so she was not our babysitter. When I went over there as a toddler, my grandfather used to smoke cigars but every time I came around, he had to stop because of my asthma and my allergy to smoke. He eventually quit smoking altogether when I was eight years old. I guess my asthma had some positive things coming from it. My grandmother was not as familiar with all my allergies as Auntie Mary, so there were several occasions in my early years when I went to her house while she was cooking seafood, and the smell permeated the house. We either had to leave, or if the weather was nice enough, I sat outside with my family.

When I was a year old, I traveled to our home country, Antigua. My father is from Antigua. I am a first-generation American. My parents were with me the whole time, so they didn't worry about me eating anything I was allergic to. We stayed at my aunt's house, so my parents shopped for groceries, and my mom prepared my food. This was the beginning of my travels. I will talk about travel and living in another country later in the book. When I was in kindergarten, I had a skin prick test for environmental allergies and was found to be allergic to pollen, ragweed, grass, cat dander, dog dander, and dust. My allergist prescribed allergy shots.

I was blessed that my mom was in the medical field, and my doctor trusted her based on experience to effectively administer allergy injections. I had them from ages six to eight years old. I attribute those allergy shots to why I have never had a sinus infection. I was able to mow the lawn as a weekly chore in high school. I was able to babysit families with cats and dogs. I never had an asthma attack. I recently did an asthma study with a local university and had a skin test for these same environmental allergens. It was reactive, so I am still allergic but not as bad as I was as a child before my allergy shots.

The allergy to dogs and cats made things tricky as a child because when I would go to friends' houses for playdates, if they had a pet, it had to be put away somewhere. I grew up in suburban Michigan. It seemed everyone had a dog or cat, if not both. My mom is also allergic to dogs and cats, so even once I was no longer having symptoms around them, she was the one that washed my clothes, so I wouldn't have the dander on my clothes when I came into the house otherwise, she would have an asthma attack.

My family took at least one major family vacation every year. We also went to New York at the end of most summers to visit my paternal grandmother. When I was in third grade, we went to Antigua, and my cousins went as well. This was an enjoyable vacation to have my cousins there with us. I knew what I could and could not eat, so I didn't need my parents with me all the time. The biggest thing for me at this age was to eat what I knew because I knew that it would be safe. This was before the internet, so all I could do was go to the grocery store once I arrived or ask questions when I was at restaurants to make sure the food was safe. When I was a kid,

Antigua did not have American fast-food chains, but now they have KFC, McDonald's, Domino's Pizza, etc. Most of the Caribbean islands have a few American chain restaurants.

When I was eight years old, my family attended a group for asthma families. It was divided with parents in one room and kids in another. We learned a lot about asthma and what to do in case of an emergency, how to live with asthma and allergies, and how to be a family with allergies.

GOING TO SCHOOL

When I was two years old, I was about to be a big sister, so my parents decided when my little sister was born it would be time for me to begin nursery school. This is something that many parents deal with everyday. The big difference for my parents was that they had a very sickly two-year-old with numerous food allergies and severe asthma. Let me remind you this was in 1978. Nowadays, you can search on google and find nut-free preschools. But then, even in 2021, it would be difficult for my parents to find a preschool because I have so many allergies.

    My mom needed a preschool close to home because of preparation for kindergarten, administering medication, and working with a long food allergy list. She researched preschools in our area and visited and interviewed the staff. I ended up at two preschools because we moved before I started elementary school. I ate breakfast, lunch, and snacks every day at school, and I had to take medication during the day as well. I started preschool at KinderCare, which was a top-rated franchise of nursery schools across the country. We moved and went to a private preschool owned by the Daughters of Charity, Seton Preschool, and Infant Child Care Center. I loved school except for naptime, but what kid likes naptime? In preschool, a chart was created to help my teachers and the staff understand my food allergies. My mother was very detailed, and it was worth it because I never had an allergic reaction to food while at school.

	NO	A Little	YES
Dairy	Milk, Cheese, Eggs		
Wheat	Bread, Cookies, Macaroni, Noodles	Saltines, Rita, Graham	
Fish	No fish		
Meat	Pork, Chicken - meat salad, Chop suey, Spaghetti, Chili		Plain meat: Beef, Lamb, Chicken, Hot dogs, Bacon
Veg.	Tomatoes - raw or cooked, Corn, Raw vegetables*		Raw lettuce only*, Cooked: Potatoes, yams, carrots, squash, beets, asparagus, green beans, peas, baked beans
Fruit	Citrus, Raw fruit *		Raw apples, pears, bananas*, Cooked or canned: peaches, pears, pineapple, prunes, apricots, applesauce
Juice	Citrus (orange), Tomato		Cranberry, apple, apricot
Other	Chocolate, Nuts		

Unfortunately, one day, my mom picked me up from school, and it was at home where an allergic reaction occurred My mom was preparing dinner, and before we could eat, she said I just started doing circles through the house from the kitchen to the dining room, living room, and family room and back again. She asked me what was wrong, but I was too young to verbalize what was happening. When I get sick, car rides would often relax me. My mom told my dad she was going to take me for a ride while he stayed home with my sister. My mom finally got me into the car, when I went into respiratory arrest. I stopped breathing. My mom yelled for my dad and told him we had to go to the emergency room. My mom is a respiratory therapist, and did I mention she used to teach CPR (Cardiopulmonary Resuscitation) classes? Well, she did. My mom performed CPR on me that night while my dad drove us to the emergency room. Auntie Mary and Uncle Harry came to the hospital to pick up my baby sister. Later, my mom realized what had transpired that night and that she had used her CPR skills on her child. She also realized that the nursery school administered my medication late while she administered the medication on time which meant I received too much medication that day. I never had another incident at school, and I made it through preschool.

I made it through preschool alive, thank goodness. For elementary school my parents wanted to send me to public school. It was only required that my mother speak to the administration before I enrolled to let them know that I have severe food allergies. I have to take medication every day, so I would need a school nurse, which in the 1980s was very common at schools. It is not the easiest thing to come by when it comes to public schools, but these are the things my mother needed to make sure were in a place to ensure that I would be safe.

I went to school. I was very excited to take the bus to school. Kindergarten was half a day, so I went to PM kindergarten, which meant I ate lunch at preschool before I went to elementary school, so there weren't any meals I needed to worry about at elementary school.

First grade is where I would have to be dropped off early and go to a program before school because my mom had to be at work at a specific time, and it was earlier than the school bus came to pick me up to attend Wood Creek Elementary School. First grade was the first time I ate lunch at school. Also, I had to ensure I took my meds ahead of lunchtime, so I went to the school nurse every day and received my medication. At the time, I was taking breathing treatments. (I will explain breathing treatments and nebulizers later). I took breathing treatments every day in the office. And then, during the winter, because of my asthma and what the cold air would do to my lungs, I couldn't play outside during recess, so I had to sit in the office during the break. Usually, I read a book or entertained the office staff, but that was what I had to do. Gym class was slightly challenging because certain activities were challenging for me to perform. There were other things I could do and the gym teacher understood and knew my limitations. I always had my emergency inhaler on hand if I did have a problem.

My father prepared my lunches pretty much every day. I rarely ate the prepared school lunches. They gave us a menu to know what was being served, and if it was something that I wanted, then my mom or my dad would give me money, and I would buy lunch, but for the most part, I usually ate what my dad prepared for me for lunch.

I knew that I had food allergies, so I wasn't trying to swap lunches with anyone or give my friends my food because I understood I had food allergies. I was really in tune with that. This was back in the day when you brought cupcakes and all that stuff to celebrate birthdays during school. I knew that I couldn't have chocolate. I knew I couldn't have nuts. I knew all the things I couldn't eat, so I usually didn't eat the cupcakes or treats that the moms brought. My teachers also knew what I could and couldn't eat so they were careful as well. The way my school was built, the bathroom was inside of the classroom, so really, my classroom was my sanctuary. In the lunchroom, I didn't have any problems. I didn't have to sit by myself away from all the kids or anything. I ate lunch with all my friends. I didn't share my lunch, and I didn't eat what they had. I guess I've always been good about washing my hands, and I didn't touch other people's property. I didn't touch other people, so I didn't have to worry about that because I have contact allergies regarding seafood, nuts, citrus fruits, and eggs. But, it has to be a cracked egg.

Before middle school, there was one final test that everyone had to take for gym class, the Presidential Physical Fitness Test. You had to run a mile in a given time, and you had to do sit-ups in a certain amount of time. I knew this test was going to be tough for me. I did run the mile, but I was the last person in my class to complete it. I do not know how long it took me. I just know that I felt like I was dying by the end of it. I finished and I remember my entire class cheered me on, and my teacher and everyone was so amazed I finished. It just took me forever to complete.

RENEE'S REMEDY

Education is vital, and no one deserves to be denied a good and quality education in spite of their health condition. Still, the parent should make the school aware of the child's health condition so, in case of an emergency, they have a plan to follow to ensure the safety of the child. The child also needs to know his or her limits to avoid any form of their triggers. You can see I know my limits, and I never tried to go beyond my limits.

GIRL SCOUT CAMP

I was a Brownie (Girl Scout) and in third grade; I was eight years old. We decided to go camping with the Brownie troop. My mom, grandmother, and aunt were all Brownies, so this was a long tradition of Girl Scouts in my family. My scout leaders knew about my asthma and allergies.

We had troop meetings and obviously, I could only eat certain foods or whatever food I brought and couldn't just eat any available food in the camp. But this time, the camping trip came the same weekend after my father had brain surgery. Even though my mom wanted to be with my dad, the scout leaders required her to accompany me at camp because they were not allowed to administer medication to the Brownies.

Camp was great! I didn't get sick because my mom was there for me and helped me get my medicine, and I had a great time. My next camping experience was when I was a mentor with Camp CEO. I spent the night, did a campfire and I didn't get sick. It was beautiful because we were out in the woods and I was able to take care of myself. I say this because not everyone will be comfortable giving medications to children.

RENEE'S REMEDY

Sometimes you have to make provisions for your child because you can't expect people, who are not health professionals, to administer medications to children.

FIFTH GRADE HOSPITALIZATION

When I was in elementary school, I went to lots of birthday parties. Many of these were slumber parties. This particular spring weekend, I attended a slumber party of a friend that I knew for a long time, so her parents were very aware of my allergies and asthma.

I had a great time at the party. The following day it was brisk outside and it was the change of season in Michigan. Change of season is when I often get sick. We were playing outside, and for some reason, I didn't have shoes or a jacket on. My mom came to pick me up and was furious. I really couldn't figure out what the big deal was. That evening I said those famous words, in our house at least, "Mommy, I can't breathe."

I ended up in the emergency room again. The doctors and nurses couldn't get my attack under control, and our local hospital did not have in-patient care, so they took me by ambulance to Children's Hospital in downtown Detroit. I spent five days in the hospital. I had a roommate who had sickle cell anemia, so she also spent a lot of time there. As a result, she kindly showed me the ropes. She had me push her in her wheelchair, and I found out they had a library, a place where we could play video games, and do all sorts of cool stuff. To date, this was my most extended hospital stay. I have never stayed in the hospital again since this incident.

RENEE'S REMEDY

Always ensure your kids know their triggers. Change of seasons is never a good time to play outside without socks and shoes. This shows you that environmental allergies can cause you to have an asthma attack and end up in the hospital just as fast as food allergies. If your child has to be hospitalized, please make sure someone can be with him/her at all times. At ten years old, I don't remember previous hospitalizations, but it was great at Children's Hospital. My mom worked in the same medical center, and there was an underground tunnel, which made it easy for her to visit often. When she wasn't in my room, one of her employees was. It would be best if you always have an advocate, and you are your children's best advocate.

I remember when I was ten years old, and we were at the mall. I am not sure what triggered it, but I started crying on a chair in the furniture department of JCPenney's at Twelve Oaks Mall in Novi, Michigan. I questioned my mom as to why I have asthma and all these allergies. My mom was sitting next to me and assured me that I would be fine and that God made no mistakes when He created me. I never asked God why I have asthma ever again. This is my thing, and I think we all have a thing. Kids with asthma and allergies need to understand their condition and their triggers. The more they know, the better they will be. This also decreases their anxiety around their condition.

URGENT CARE EXPERIENCE

I had an asthma attack, and I was gasping when my mom called the pediatrician. He had an urgent care facility that was close to the house. He advised her to bring me there. My mom and I got in the car without anyone else in my family. This was unusual because when I had my attacks we usually went to the emergency room as a family. I think my mom thought my doctor would treat me and send us back home, so there was no need for everyone to go. Also, this was not a middle of the night attack, but this was an early evening one.

I was ten years old at the time. I remember this episode clearly like it was yesterday. We got to the urgent care, and my mom got me inside, and I sat down on a bean bag because that is what they had in the lobby. I kept trying to get comfortable, but I just couldn't. My mom was at the counter talking to the medical staff. All I know is that my mom came back, and they called her back to the desk to ask her more questions and to complete more paperwork. My mom returned and told me she was going to get the car, then return for me. This was a bit odd to me. She then said, "Reneé, we are going to the emergency room."

On our ride to the emergency room, my mom was calling my name. I can still hear her saying it, "Reneé! Reneé!" and I could not answer. I tried to moan, but that didn't come out either. I couldn't move either, so she could at least see that I could hear her by responding in some way.

My mom pulled the car over and shook me. She called my name and made sure she looked into my eyes to be sure that I was still alive. Then she turned her attention back to the driver's seat so that we could get back on the road. When we arrived at the emergency room, they took me in immediately as they always did. Most of the time, when you go to the emergency room, they send you to triage, where they sort out patients according to their medical needs and ask questions about what brought one into the hospital. I honestly don't know if I knew what triage was until med school. I was always taken right back to be seen bypassing triage.

RENEE'S REMEDY

Always remain calm and try not to be overwhelmed. My mom remained calm throughout this entire situation, which allowed me to do the same. I remember this incident like it was yesterday. I felt terrible because I was really struggling to breathe, and my mom was doing everything in her power to get me the help I so desperately needed. She did the absolute right thing by leaving that urgent care center when it was apparent they were going to take too long to treat me. When breathing concerns are involved, time is not on your side. Act quickly but calmly.

THE FUNERAL

My first memory of attending a funeral was when I was in the sixth grade, eleven years old. The person in the casket didn't look old, and when I say didn't look old, she didn't look like my grandmother. She looked like she could have been my mom. The person in the casket was, in fact, young (in her thirties or forties). She was my cousin. I learned that she died from an asthma attack. Now, at my age knowing I had asthma, that scared me out of my mind to think that this could kill me. My mom had told me that I needed to take this seriously because people die from not breathing. I was a typical kid who didn't believe everything her parents told her. Now, I was face to face with precisely what my mom had been teaching me all along.

I later heard the story of what happened to her. She had an asthma attack, couldn't breathe, and collapsed in the presence of her child, but her child was too young to know how to call for help, so the child just lay down and fell asleep. I was told that they discovered that the child, of course, woke up and the mother had died. I realized what my mother kept saying was true, and from then on, I decided that I wanted to enjoy my life, and I understood how important taking care of my asthma was to keep breathing. I knew how important it was to say, "Mommy, I can't breathe" so that she could make sure that I got air to breathe. I was also a little nervous about ever living alone., I always tried to pay very close attention to my asthma so that I wouldn't get in such a situation.

RENEE'S REMEDY

Never take anything for granted especially if you have asthma. Be alert and pay attention at all times no matter the age.

OLIVER!

My sister and I attended day camp every summer while my parents were working. One of my favorite camps was at the local community college. We would have classes like we were students. I had a musical theater class that ended in a stage play. In my first year of the camp, the play was Oliver! I was so excited to be one of Fagin's boys and could sing and dance.

The opening night, my mom took my sister and me to a restaurant that I had never visited, but my parents had eaten there and ordered take-out. I ordered my usual chicken fingers and fries. My food came, and I took a bite. I immediately told my mom my tongue was itching. She looked over my shoulder and noticed the people that had ordered fish were nibbling away at what looked just like the chicken that was ordered. It turns out they had fried the fish and the chicken in the same fryer. We immediately had to leave and go home to get my breathing machine and then go to the theater. I was backstage all night taking my breathing treatments in between scenes. My mom later went to the restaurant and explained what they did and how dangerous it was. I don't think I ever ate there again.

RENEE'S REMEDY

When eating out, you need to ask questions. Definitely teach your children to advocate for themselves to survive in this world when they leave the nest, which is not a world that is necessarily friendly to people with food allergies. The one thing that I had was my sister. She would taste everything before I did. She is younger than me and couldn't necessarily tell me what I was allergic to, but she would say, "No, you can't eat this." The more people who know about your child's allergies, the more people can look out for your child. I understand that not all kids have a sibling like I did, but their classmates, cousins, and friends need to be aware. All my friends knew I had food allergies, and even if they didn't remember all of my allergies, they would ask before I came over or before they offered me food.

BABYSITTING

When I was in fifth grade, I was ten years old and began reading "The Babysitter's Club" by Ann M. Martin. I loved that series of books. I read all of them, and I really wanted to be a part of a babysitters' club. Unfortunately, at that age I didn't have other friends that babysat. By the time I was twelve my mom was able to find a class at the library that taught kids how to be good babysitters and what to do in case of emergency while babysitting.

I took that class, and then I started watching younger cousins, and I mean, they were infants to toddlers that I watched. I was a latchkey kid, so my sister and I usually stayed home for a couple of hours after school together, but my sister is only two and a half years younger than me. , so that wasn't really babysitting. Slowly but surely, my neighbors started calling, and my mom said I could say yes as long as she was going to be home and available if something happened.

I babysat in my neighborhood, and not too far from my house. I think the most I've traveled was maybe three to four miles. The parents came and picked me up, and they would bring me home at the end of the night. When I babysat I had to feed the children, and that wasn't a problem because I brought my own food. If the parents said, feel free to eat if it was something I could eat, I would eat , and sometimes they would have me order food, and I would order a pizza for delivery. I could eat pizza. One time when I arrived to babysit, the mom had been frying fish. I could smell it as soon as I walked in the house, and needless to say, I couldn't babysit that day. My mom was able to pinch hit for me, and that actually might have been the first day my sister started babysitting too, so we had our own babysitters' club.

When I was a little girl, my babysitter was asthmatic, and she was terrific, and to this day, she is still a wonderful person. My babysitter, Dr. Laina Callentine, then Shaw is a pediatric ER doctor and to this day we remain in touch. She told stories that came alive and she is the reason I became a storyteller. Storytelling is the category that I competed in forensics in middle school and high school. Dr. Shaw understood my asthma because she had asthma. She also understood what I had to do in case of an emergency. She knew about the medications and action plans, which was why she was the perfect babysitter for me.

When I think of all the kids I babysat, only one, I believe may have had asthma. If possible, find a babysitter that your child can look up to. Lainna played basketball with severe asthma and I danced. That makes me get rid of excuses because if she could do it, I could do it. It was great to see her in action and have her as an influence in my life, and she may have had some influence in me becoming a doctor. Lainna was terrific.

RENEE'S REMEDY

Matchmaking your child with a babysitter who has something in common is a perfect fit. Seeing someone thriving with asthma, shows what is possible.

PAPER ROUTE

It is no surprise that I am an entrepreneur now because when I was younger, I knew money meant something to me. I knew that I wanted to earn extra money, so I decided to get a paper route when I was in the eighth grade. Now, I knew paper routes were demanding, which is why I opted for the Farmington Observer & Eccentric route, which was only two days a week, Mondays and Thursdays. My route was just my subdivision, so it wasn't a massive route with only thirty houses. I foolishly thought that I could do this route myself, but my sister helped me, thankfully. We got baskets on our bikes, rolled the newspapers together, and rode our bikes, tossing the newspapers onto our customer's driveways. That was great in warm weather but then winter came. I think I hadn't thought that far ahead. I, of course, have severe asthma and couldn't be outside just riding a bike in the cold weather, so my mother had to drive, and we had to throw the papers from the car window. My sister no longer wanted to be bothered with the paper route, so it was all on me. I retained the route for about three years and that was my first little job.

RENEE'S REMEDY

Be mindful of the impact of weather on your health. Choose a job wisely.

MY DANCING DAYS

As a child, it was apparent I could not participate in athletics. To be honest I don't think I really had an interest in them anyway. I guess that worked out in my favor, but I did have an interest in the arts. I then started dancing, without having any problems with my breathing. Dancing never pushed me to use an emergency inhaler or any other medication, so I was okay.

I was so good at dancing that I became a part of the competition group at Gayle's Dancephase. We traveled to competitions as a team, and of course, our travel schedule didn't necessarily go along with my parent's work schedule. My dance teacher was okay taking me along, and sometimes my sister traveled with me. Without my parents and really no chaperone for me, my sister reminded me to take my medications, but she also assisted when necessary. She was aware of my allergies. I was in middle school going into high school when I was participating in dancing competitions. I was old enough to speak up and take care of myself. My teacher and her family would make sure that I got moved right away if the dancing organizing team placed me in a moldy hotel room.

Mind you, I'm also allergic to mold and mildew, so it was great to have adults around who knew of my allergies. So, dancing is the sport I participated in for a long time, and we traveled all over the country for competitions. Like I said earlier, my parents did not always come along. Nevertheless, I never felt like I wasn't safe or something could have happened because I always had my breathing machine. I had my emergency inhaler. I had my daily medication. At this point, I was taking pills every day. And I always traveled with my prescriptions. I took care of myself, and it was great. Everything was fine with dancing.

RENEE'S REMEDY

Do what you enjoy. Make certain you plan and prepare with any essential items you might need.

SLEEPOVER CAMP

Most of the kids I went to middle school with went to sleepover camps during the summer. Of course, that was kind of tricky for me because of my asthma, and I was on daily nebulizer treatment plus pills, so it would be challenging for me to attend sleepover camp. Somebody would have to be responsible to administer all of my medications. Plus, being outside every day and being exposed to environmental allergens such as grass, weeds, trees etc. could be dangerous. My mom found out about the asthma camp. The asthma camp wasn't called that, but that's what we called it in our house, the camp was staffed by respiratory therapists and doctors. They gave kids their treatments and their medications around the clock, and they understood about food allergies and environmental allergies because this camp was a sleepover camp in the woods. I was excited when my mom told me about this camp. The camp was for one week and it was a chance to experience a sleepover camp in a safe environment. Not only did they want to expose us to the camp experience and environment but they also wanted us to try foods that we wouldn't ordinarily eat. The staff, who were all medical professionals, said we would be fine because we had the medicine and equipment if anyone had an anaphylaxis reaction. I said to myself "these people are trying to convince me to eat stuff I can't eat" and I thought they had lost their minds. I've been sick so many times before, I knew what it felt like not to be able to breathe, so therefore I didn't want to be ill and not be able to breathe. I've said before I had allergy shots when I was in elementary school, since then I never really had any problems in the environment, so as far as trees and woods, I was ok. It was just the foods that I was concerned about, and they, of course, had food I could eat. In the morning, they like to have oatmeal, and at the time, I still wasn't eating oatmeal, so I thought that they were crazy trying to convince me to eat it. I ended up going to asthma camp for a couple of years and this is where I was first re-introduced to oatmeal in my diet and I loved it! Fast forward to today. I eat oatmeal almost daily, so they were right. I was wrong and I can eat oatmeal. In college I started using skim milk because my mom told me she felt it would be alright for me to drink or use in my oatmeal. I drank skim milk until 2017 when I took milk out of my diet. I found flax milk by Good Karma foods to be delicious. The only problem was that it was hard to find in my neighborhood grocery store. I then discovered Oatly, which is sold in Whole Foods and Target. Then, in 2019, Chobani came out with their oat milk and it is delicious and widely available at my neighborhood grocery store. I have not had skim milk since 2017 and I can't feel or hear the congestion in my lungs any more. No more dairy milk for me.

RENEE'S REMEDY

Even when you think you know everything, there's something new to learn. Be open.

HIGH SCHOOL

When I was in high school, my parents left for work early in the morning, and my sister and I were responsible for getting ourselves to the school bus. One day during my freshman year of high school, I went to school knowing I was having trouble breathing. I just figured I would get better throughout the day and be fine. Unfortunately, things never went as I thought. My best friend, Selam, called my mom from the payphone and told her that I was wheezing, short of breath and hadn't been active or concentrating at school. My mom told her to put me on the phone, and, at this point, I could barely talk without taking breaths. I asked my mom to bring my nebulizer so that I could take a treatment and continue my classes. After taking a treatment I still was not able to breathe well enough to remain in school and so we had to go to the emergency room. I begged my mother to take me back to school after I was discharged from the emergency room.

I was opposed to going to the hospital because, by the time I was in high school, I had figured out that the only thing that the doctors could use to break my asthma attacks was steroids. Specifically, they used Prednisone, which has side effects, one of the main ones being moon face. This means my nose spreads across my face, and my face gets very round. Of course, I am only on a short course of steroids, but it takes a little while for that to go away. You can imagine a fourteen-year-old being very vain and not wanting to change her appearance. Typically, this is a critical age where teens are concerned about appearance more than health. As I write this book, I realize how stupid this was for me to feel this way about my looks, but I was a fourteen-year-old teenaged girl. Please grant me some grace. I am older and wiser. I realize it's better to have a moon face than to be in a casket with a pretty face.

RENEE'S REMEDY

This is where an Asthma Action Plan (AAP) can be beneficial. I was a freshman in high school, so I was old enough to know what this was and how to abide by it. An AAP is a written, individualized worksheet that shows you the steps to take to keep your asthma from getting worse. A peak flow meter is a portable, inexpensive, hand-held device used to measure how air flows from your lungs in one "fast blast." In other words, the meter measures your ability to push air out of your lungs.

ASTHMA ACTION PLAN

Asthma and Allergy Foundation of America
aafa.org

Name:	Date:
Doctor:	Medical Record #:
Doctor's Phone #: Day	Night/Weekend
Emergency Contact:	
Doctor's Signature:	

The colors of a traffic light will help you use your asthma medicines.

GREEN means Go Zone!
Use preventive medicine.

YELLOW means Caution Zone!
Add quick-relief medicine.

RED means Danger Zone!
Get help from a doctor.

Personal Best Peak Flow: _____

GO — Use these daily controller medicines:

You have *all* of these:
- Breathing is good
- No cough or wheeze
- Sleep through the night
- Can work & play

Peak flow: from ___ to ___

MEDICINE	HOW MUCH	HOW OFTEN/WHEN

For asthma with exercise, take:

CAUTION — Continue with green zone medicine and add:

You have *any* of these:
- First signs of a cold
- Exposure to known trigger
- Cough
- Mild wheeze
- Tight chest
- Coughing at night

Peak flow: from ___ to ___

MEDICINE	HOW MUCH	HOW OFTEN/WHEN

CALL YOUR ASTHMA CARE PROVIDER.

DANGER — Take these medicines and call your doctor now.

Your asthma is getting worse fast:
- Medicine is not helping
- Breathing is hard & fast
- Nose opens wide
- Trouble speaking
- Ribs show (in children)

Peak flow: reading below ___

MEDICINE	HOW MUCH	HOW OFTEN/WHEN

GET HELP FROM A DOCTOR NOW! Your doctor will want to see you right away. It's important! If you cannot contact your doctor, go directly to the emergency room. **DO NOT WAIT.**
Make an appointment with your asthma care provider within two days of an ER visit or hospitalization.

COLLEGE DAYS

I am glad to say that the rest of my high school years were full of usual teenage angst. I was active in the school plays, on the forensic team and traveled to school competitions. I got my driver's license and a car at sixteen and started eating out a lot more with friends. Most of my friends let me choose where we ate because of my allergies, but I always made sure I could find something on the menu.

When I decided I would become a Michigan State University (MSU) Spartan, my mom made sure I would thrive living away from home. I was registered as a disabled student. This allowed me some excellent services to live and attend the most prominent Big Ten university campus in the country. Because of my environmental allergies, it was not advisable for me to open windows because pollen, dust, or weeds could blow into my room. The dormitories lacked air conditioning in the students' rooms which triggered my breathing difficulties when the outdoor temperature and humidity increased on the warm weather days. The university approved of me having an air conditioning unit. My dad purchased and installed the unit. I was allowed to have a car on campus as a freshman, and I was allotted a parking space at each of the buildings where I had classes. I also had access to the handicap bus if I couldn't drive to class, or I could call and get door-to-door service.

My mother never thought I would be able to go away to college because I was so sickly. Thankfully, as I got older, my asthma improved. Improved meaning the medical community had better drugs to control it, and I had fewer and fewer attacks. I usually got sick during the change of seasons, particularly during October and April, but it didn't require me to go to the hospital.

In my freshmen year, I was so excited to get to MSU and be on my own. I thought I had everything, but I forgot some asthma equipment, such as my breathing machine. I had to call my parents in the middle of the night with my least favorite saying, "Mommy, I can't breathe."

Asthma attacks often happened at night, which is when I would get sick ninety percent of the time. I told them what was happening, and they came to campus with the equipment. My suitemates had cigarette smoke coming from their room, and it had caused me breathing problems.

RENEE'S REMEDY

Communication is the key. When I moved into my dorm room, I should have had a conversation with my suitemates. We shared a bathroom, which meant that anything that happened in their room would come under the door to my room. If I told them that my oxygen tank could blow up due to the smoke, they probably wouldn't have been smoking in their room. My room was deemed a handicap room because of my asthma. I had an air conditioner, which no other dorm rooms had. If they had known this move-in day, they might have chosen a different suitemate.

I CAN'T BREATHE

I was registered as a handicapped student on MSU's campus because of the severity of my asthma, so I had a car my entire time there. It gave me access to parking and driving to all my classes; no students could drive and park on campus until after school hours.

One day I recall giving a friend a ride home, and on my way back to the dorm, I had this coughing attack. I dropped her off for what was maybe a five-minute drive away. Apparently, according to a campus police officer, I ran a stop sign, so he pulled me over. I rolled my window down. I think it was that night when the air got into my lungs and began a reaction, and I started coughing uncontrollably while trying to talk to him. I then recognized I was gasping and couldn't catch my breath. I gave him my information, and while he was in his car, I got out of mine because I was feeling suffocated. I really couldn't breathe. I continued coughing. I told the officer I couldn't breathe. I asked him if I could go get my inhaler because I felt as if I was dying. I pointed to my dorm room window to show him where I was headed. He said he was aware, but that didn't encourage him to expedite what he was doing. Remember, I was registered with the university as a handicapped student, so I had unique stickers on my car signifying this. I also have a handicapped placard. This incident was clearly about something else that we will save for another book.

It seemed that he took the longest I had ever seen for a traffic stop for some reason. I was declining quickly. I began leaning on the hood of my car for support so I could try to inhale, and he insisted on writing me the ticket. I received the ticket and parked the car. The stop was literally at the foot of the parking lot behind my dorm. I went upstairs and got my meds. Later, I decided to go to court to fight the ticket for no other reason than to report this officer for his behavior during a time when I had a medical emergency. I went to court with my medical records in tow. They were, at the time, about ten inches thick! I was ready to state my case. I never got the chance; the officer didn't show up to court, so the ticket was thrown out.

RENEE'S REMEDY

Never leave home without your emergency inhaler. I know better, and this rarely happens anymore. The intelligent thing to do is strategically place inhalers in your car, bag, bedside, etc. I know what you are going to say, "Insurance won't allow you to have so many inhalers." Please ask your doctor if they have samples to dispense. I do not have a bracelet that states I have asthma or food allergies. I honestly do not believe it would have helped in this situation. This officer was not listening to me, not being able to catch my breath. He didn't even have the decency to call an ambulance for me because, at that point, I was in desperate need of help.

BANANA MUFFINS

I lived in Wilson Hall my entire time at MSU. Considering all of my allergies, I could always eat on campus, if not my dormitory, then someone else's. This Sunday morning was no different than any other. I got up late and went to the cafeteria for breakfast. I was so excited they had banana muffins. In my opinion, their banana muffins were not as good as mine, but they were pretty darn close.

I advanced in the line and picked up my food. I sat alone. I pulled the cupcake wrapper off my muffin and dissected it. I ate a crumb that was barely visible to the naked eye. I immediately felt my throat get warm., I had an allergic reaction. I don't know if I disposed of the tray because I ran out of there and went back to my room. I immediately took some Benadryl. Why didn't I use the EpiPen, you might ask? I had exams the next day, and the directions on the EpiPen say as soon as you inject yourself, you need to go to the emergency room. I didn't have time for that, so I called my mom and a friend who lived two floors up from me. I left them messages because they were at church. During the call, I left a message, letting them know on the phone what happened. Benadryl makes a person sleepy, and I fell asleep for a few hours right after taking it. I was awakened when my mom called. "Reneé, we just got home from church and heard your message. Are you ok?" My mom, of course, asked why I didn't use the EpiPen. I told her the exact same thing about my exam and not having time to sit in the emergency room. And she quickly reminded me if my throat closed, I would be dead. I will always love my voice of reason. That's my mommy.

RENEE'S REMEDY

Always ensure whatever you're eating does not have your allergen. You should inquire as to what ingredients are included in the food . This happened in my dorm cafeteria, so I just went back to my room and took an antihistamine. Today, it would have been advised to use the Epinephrine Auto-Injector. My mom has always said I lived on the edge. I was a college student, and I was studying for an exam the next day. I guess my line of thinking was if the antihistamine didn't work, I would go to the emergency room. The other lesson is when in doubt, eat crumbs. Suppose I had bitten into the muffin like I usually would have done. I definitely would have been in the emergency room because there was one of my allergens present, and the more I consumed, the worse off I would have been.

CLASS OF 1999

I graduated from MSU in 1999, when I graduated from undergrad, several of my friends earned their degrees at the same time. As a result, I had lots of graduation parties to attend. I went to my friends' parties and had a great time.

My sister accompanied me. She was a good sidekick. When it was time to eat, I always found food I wasn't allergic to. My sister is a foodie, so she was good no matter what. I didn't eat dessert because I didn't see anything I could eat safely. I went to take a drink of my beverage, and my sister said, "Oh, no, Renee! I drank your drink, and I ate carrot cake with nuts." I told her if we have to leave early because I am sick, she is in big trouble! "You need to go and make sure my cup does not go empty so that I can rinse this out of my system immediately!" I recalled excitedly telling her.

RENEE'S REMEDY

Remember, I told you about my amazing little sister, my taste tester for many years? In this story, you see she almost caused me to get sick. Didn't your mother ever tell you not to drink after other people? With food allergies, this message is essential. You just never know what a person ate or had to drink. This lack of knowledge can easily cause you to end up with an allergic reaction. This book is called "Mommy, I Can't Breathe," but for any person of age, who is reading this, please don't kiss everyone with an open mouth and tongue if you have no knowledge of what they have been eating. Something as simple as kissing could also cause an allergic reaction. Perhaps I need to write another book for adolescents and adults on how to handle these situations. What do you think?

DAD'S COOKING

In 1999, I graduated from MSU with a bachelor's of science degree in physiology. For me, this basically meant that I needed to go to graduate school or teach. My plan was always to go to medical school. I needed to improve my GPA before applying to become a competitive applicant, so I attended Wayne State University in Detroit for a year before going to medical school. This was a great plan. I got to stay with my parents at our family home for a year. I soon learned that I was infringing upon my father's territory.

More than a few times, he cooked seafood, and then I would come home from class, and my lungs would sense it before I even smelled it. I usually came home and went straight to the computer, which was in the library on the opposite end of the house from the kitchen. I would close the door. I then started hearing this noise and quickly figured out what I called my "inner whistle," my wheezing. My dad would promptly open all the doors and windows to air out the house. I would take a breathing treatment to stop the attack from being a full-blown attack.

RENEE'S REMEDY

I grew up with my mom preparing seafood. She cooked it on the deck or when I was not at home and then aired it out of the house before I returned. The lesson here is that if your child is allergic to the smell of something that's being cooked, make sure you open windows and doors so that the scent clears before that child arrives. Even if it is wintertime in the Midwest. Air out the house so that the person does not inhale scents from the allergen; I understand that I am the only person with severe food allergies in my family, so now, as an adult, I accept and appreciate that they still eat what they want regardless of my allergies. The real world will make it necessary for me to understand how to navigate eating in public and private spaces with people who will consume things that I cannot eat.

ASTHMA STUDIES

In 2012, I was made aware of an asthma study. I have been doing asthma studies with the University of Chicago for the last several years, hoping that whatever information they can get from me is helpful to create new medications or find out why asthma attacks happen at night. I did a study that was checking whether my sleep patterns have something to do with asthma attacks. I've actually tested out other medications, so it has been really interesting to participate. If you're reading this and you're an asthmatic, or you're the parent of a child who is asthmatic, I encourage you to try and participate in these studies. You will meet doctors who will follow you along the way, who could ultimately change your life. It was shortly after one of the last studies that I found out that I no longer had to take ADVAIR. I was able to give my allergy and immunology doctor all of the testing results from the study. Of course, there is always payment for your gas and parking as well as for your time. The study drugs you receive will be given for free.

RENEE'S REMEDY

Be aware of possible asthma studies and be open to participating. You never know how this will change your life from the experience and by the doctors you meet.

SEAFOOD RESTAURANT OUTING

When I was younger, my mom would sometimes travel for work. She would leave us home with my padre, who is not necessarily a great cook. My padre is an island man, and he loves seafood.

We would often go to a popular seafood chain restaurant in our neighborhood. Now, I know you are thinking, how did I go to a seafood restaurant when I am allergic to seafood? The difference here is that I could never smell seafood cooking at the restaurant. My dad would order seafood, and I would order my usual chicken fingers and fries. So, when I was home from medical school one Christmas break, my friend suggested we go to this seafood chain restaurant. The waitress brought the breadbasket and I remember I was famished. I didn't usually eat from the breadbasket, but I decided to give them a try. Unfortunately, due to some cross-contamination between the bread and my friend eating seafood with her hands, I had a horrible allergic reaction. This was the first time I had terrible gastrointestinal (GI) symptoms, which is code for I vomited for hours at my friend's boyfriend's brand new house. Talk about being embarrassed. I had gotten it on the wallpaper and the bathroom floor. I will never forget that reaction. It took me nearly ten years to go back to that restaurant. Let's say I was scared for a while, and rightfully so.

RENEE'S REMEDY

Cross contamination is real. When dining, please make sure everyone at the table is aware of the person with food allergies. It is probably best if anything is family-style, that you tell the waiter or whoever is serving that your child needs his/her own portions instead of sharing others. For instance, when a breadbasket is involved, it is best for the person with allergies to have his/her own, so this person doesn't have to worry about people eating with their hands and causing cross-contamination. When dishes are served, the utensils cannot cross from one dish to another. I handle this situation best because my food is on a separate serving dish.

BUYING EGGS

I have always been allergic to eggs, but I can eat them cooked in food as long as there are not too many. Foods such as cheesecake and French vanilla ice cream have too many. When I was in medical school, I bought some eggs, and I was so worried about dropping them that I handled them with extra care. I remember removing them from the car and holding the carton close to my chest as I strolled to my apartment. About twenty minutes later, my chest was itching and was hot. I looked down at my shirt and noticed something was on it. I then realized I should check the eggs. Most people accustomed to buying them check the carton before purchase, but I neglected to do so. One of the eggs was cracked, and I got egg whites on my shirt, which, of course, got on my skin. I was beginning to have an asthma attack because of this. I took a shower, grabbed some Benadryl, and lived to see another day.

RENEE'S REMEDY

Make sure you do not allow your children to touch things they are allergic to because, more than likely, they will react. I can touch oranges because they have skin. But once that is removed, I do not touch them. If I do touch an orange, I wash my hands immediately with soap and water. This is how I can cook and bake with eggs. I also used to fish with my dad when I was a kid, and I would do the same thing. After taking the fish off the hook, I would immediately wash my hands. If I had so much as touched my face or put my hands in my mouth, I would have been sick.

ACCIDENTAL EPIPEN

I was in medical school, and I have had an EpiPen since its inception. I was about ten years old when I received my first EpiPen. I don't know what got into me, but I was curious about it one day after class.

I pulled it out and was staring at it, trying to figure out how it worked. In that instance, I figured out how it worked. I stabbed myself in the palm of my hand with the huge needle. I quickly pulled it out and handled myself.

RENEE'S REMEDY

I was an adult when this mishap took place, and I am still in shock that it happened, but I guess curiosity killed the cat. The most embarrassing part is that my mom told my allergist what I did. Get your kids a trainer so they can practice and see how this works. A trainer device wasn't available when I was younger. I'm glad things have changed.

IS CHICKEN CURRY EQUAL TO CURRY CHICKEN?

I went to an Indian restaurant with one of my classmates in England, and I ordered chicken curry, which I presumed would be similar to curry chicken in my West Indian culture. I enjoyed my meal, but then I had some stomach symptoms.

I kept going to the bathroom because, like I said, I was having some symptoms associated with an upset stomach. I kept having diarrhea, not throwing up.. We left the restaurant once we were done with the meal. At this point, I had never had diarrhea with my allergic reactions. It was always my throat swelling and then wheezing. So, we had dinner and then left. We were talking on the sidewalk near the outside of the cab. I vomited on the sidewalk and felt so much better because I got it out of my system. After that, I just kept talking to her, but I noticed that the saliva did not go back down my throat. I realized that my throat was closing, and I told her I had to go. I had to get in another cab to get home right away and take Benadryl because I was about to have an allergic reaction.

The next day my mom told me, "You should really go back to the restaurant and find out what was in that dish." I went, and a man who worked there told me what was in it. I couldn't think of any of the ingredients that he stated I might have been allergic to. However,

I thought I heard him mention yogurt. To this day, I don't know what it was that caused the reaction, but I now steer clear of Indian curry because of that incident. As you can see, the running theme here is I only need one terrible experience for me to realize certain things I should just leave alone. I can eat many foods without a problem, so I don't have any issue with missing a few items.

RENEE'S REMEDY

Before this trip, I had only eaten Naan bread from Indian restaurants. I should have asked questions before I assumed that all curry chicken or chicken curry is the same. My rule of thumb for thirty-plus years was no sauces. Just eat it plain. Seasonings are great, but sauces have lots of ingredients that if someone forgets to tell you, this lack of information could be the cause of an allergic reaction. Unless I make it or I see it made or know the chef, I am back to that rule of thumb. If you can taste it and have a very sophisticated palate, and figure out what the ingredients are, you can feel comfortable feeding this to your child.

LUNCH WITH MY MENTOR

I was in town from medical school and visited my favorite obstetrician and gynecologist, Dr. Patrice Harold. (Just ask Oprah. That story is for another book.) She said, let's go to lunch. We can go to a Middle Eastern restaurant down the street.

In my adult life, I have tried to be more open to trying new foods. Middle Eastern was not in my old palette of fried chicken fingers and French fries. I ordered chicken shawarma and rice. The rice had some brown pieces, but I just assumed it was like wild rice. Wrong!!!! Those were pine nuts, and I immediately began to react. She took me back to her office and offered me an antihistamine for the reaction. This was the last time I ate Middle Eastern food. As I have mentioned before, sometimes you just have to decide that you need to stay away from certain cuisines or restaurants for safety reasons.

RENEE'S REMEDY

This serves as another reminder to remain calm. I was reacting, but this time I could talk and think clearly. This is another situation where I should have used my Epinephrine Auto-Injector, but, I will be honest, I didn't start carrying it until about five years later. I didn't even have an antihistamine in my purse. The biggest lesson here was that I was eating a type of food that I had never eaten before. I did not ask questions. I just assumed that what I ordered was safe. If you are going to try something new, ask lots of questions before you eat. The same thing goes for environmental allergies. If you are traveling to someplace with different altitudes, or are surrounded by bodies of water that you are not used to experiencing, you need to know this ahead of time and talk to your doctor about handling it so as not to get sick. Also, when visiting people's homes, be sure to ask if they have pets if that is among your allergies.

ICE SCREAM YOU SCREAM

My sister told me about this new franchise where they make the ice cream on a slab with incredible ingredients in front of you, and I hadn't made it to Chicago yet, so I had never experienced it.

When we went to New York for my graduation, there was one in Times Square. I was so excited. My sister told me all about this apple pie ice cream. I knew that was exactly what I was going to get when I went in there. I had it, and this was everything my sister had described.

I went back to Chicago, and low and behold; we had the ice cream shop not far from where I lived. I planned a hair wash day and purchased this dessert beforehand and placed it in my freezer. While I sat under the dryer, I planned to enjoy my ice cream. I got myself all set up and got the ice cream out of the freezer. I took one spoonful and immediately knew I was going to be in trouble.

My throat started itching, and I immediately took Benadryl. I knew that if I told my mom and sister, they would say I had no business eating ice cream anyway because of the calories. Don't tell them I told you, but when I started reacting, the first thing I thought of was that is God telling me I had no business eating ice cream! I lived to see another day, and in about a week, I finally confessed to them. I also finally said out loud I will never eat at a slab ice cream shop again.

RENEE'S REMEDY

The lesson here is that not everything is for everybody. I was twenty-nine years old when I had that ice cream, which was the last time I dined there. I cannot take the risk of the slab not being clean enough for me to be safe. I have visited an ice cream place that mixed the ice cream as you ordered, and they had signs posted that stated if you have food allergies, let them know because they would bring out brand new utensils to make your ice cream. I felt seen and heard, but this is not common, so please be careful.

DESSERT ANYONE?

My friend said," let's go to dinner." We chose a restaurant, a franchise I was very familiar with due to my college days. I tell you this because we would eat there often. I had eaten a lot of Applebee's during those college years. This means this is where I have options on the menu that I can eat without problems. I ate my entrée with no issues. Here comes the dessert.

So, as a rule of thumb, I rarely eat desserts at restaurants because I am usually allergic to them. There was an apple dish on the menu. I was so excited!!! I asked the waitresses if there were nuts in it. She said no. I ordered it, ate a spoonful or two, and then I saw something! I asked my friend if that was a nut? He said it was. I told him I was allergic. He started sweating and panicking. I told him to calm down. I informed him that I was still talking to him and breathing, so I was okay.

RENEE'S REMEDY

Please inspect your food when it is not something you usually order. Ask questions and look it over. If I had just run my spoon inside of the dish, I would have seen the nuts before eating any. Thank goodness I ate a small bite. Once again, a small bite saved me from a terrible reaction.

FOOD ALLERGY EXPO

One Sunday morning, I happened to see online that there was a Food Allergy Expo that had come to town and it was very close to where I lived. So, I thought I should go and it was the last day, so I think they had maybe three hours left when I finally could get myself together to leave. When I arrived, it was marvelous to see the many foods that were allergen-free. Many of them are brands that you see at the grocery store all the time, but they also had a variety that was absent of allergens. Many of these products were not available in the U.S. you have to get them in Canada or someplace else. But there was one particular product that I tried that day that was available in the U.S., and now it's widespread. It was sun butter. Sunbutter is basically a butter spread made with sunflower seeds, it is very similar to peanut butter in color, texture, and smell. I will never forget the gentleman at the table with sun butter trying to convince me to try it. They had Mallard crackers there that you could use to try the Sunbutter. Well, not the crackers he had. I think they were just plain saltine crackers, and it just looked and smelled so much like peanut butter. I said no, and he kept trying to convince me that I was not allergic to it because it was sunflower seeds, and if I had sunflower seeds, I would be fine. Finally, I said OK, I tried it, it tasted good, and I didn't get sick. I said, well, where do I buy this? At the time, Sunbutter was only sold at Whole Foods. Now you can buy it at most grocery stores. But remember I said that this was the last day of the expo, so they were closing out and cleaning up to leave all the extra samples. He gave them to me to enjoy until I was able to purchase my own. Sunbutter now has all sorts of varieties like crunchy and chocolate. When recipes call for peanut butter, I use Sunbutter instead, and I make little sandwiches with Sunbutter and jam or jelly and for the first time, I had my version of a peanut butter and jelly sandwich.

RENEE'S REMEDY

Educate yourself about the many foods you can eat that are allergen-free. Search for possible Food Allergy Expos that you might be able to attend.

HALF MARATHON

My sister ran the Disney World Half Marathon by herself in January 2009, so I promised her that I would go with her the next time she set out to do this. I didn't want her to do it alone. However, I fooled around and let the 5K walk that I planned to do, sell out. As a result, I had to commit to run the half marathon.

I started training in June 2009 by preparing for my first 5k, the Long Run, on September 11, 2009. I always carried my inhaler with me, and I would usually take a few puffs before I started any rigorous activity. I had it with me on this day to ensure that I wouldn't have any trouble when I finished.

In the past, I wasn't a runner at all, but if I did decide to go for a sprint, I would be winded for so long because I just couldn't catch my breath. When January 2010 came around, and it was time to run the Disney World Half Marathon, I had run two 5k races and two 10k races. I never used my inhaler while I was running, but it was always handy. I didn't know that there would be pacers, and they threw me off with my timing, so I did not complete the half marathon, but I did manage to run 8.4 miles!

RENEE'S REMEDY

Exercise can help get your asthma under control. This one still surprises me to this day. I would have never thought that simple exercise would drastically change my Pulmonary Function Test, which are noninvasive tests that show how well the lungs are working. The tests measure lung volume, capacity, rates of flow, and gas exchange. This information can help your doctor diagnose and decide the treatment of asthma and other lung disorders. According to the medical community, some types of exercise can reduce or prevent asthma symptoms. These exercises work by making your lungs stronger without worsening inflammation. This is the explanation of what has happened to my lungs. The exercises best for asthma involve short bursts of exertion and low intensity. These exercises do not overwork your lungs, so they are less likely to cause asthma symptoms: Swimming, hiking, recreational biking, short-distance track and field, baseball, volleyball, gymnastics, golf, and football. The reason that these activities are suitable for asthma is because of the following reasons:

Reduce inflammation. Though asthma inflames the airways, regular exercise can actually decrease inflammation. It works by reducing inflammatory proteins, which improves how your airways respond to exercise.

- Improve lung capacity. The more you work out, the more your lungs get used to consuming oxygen. This decreases how hard your body must work on breathing daily.

- Strengthen muscles. When your muscles are strong, the body functions more efficiently during everyday activities.

- Improve cardiovascular fitness. Exercise improves the overall conditioning of the heart, improving blood flow and the delivery of oxygen.

Over time, working out can help your airways build up a tolerance to exercise. This makes it easier for your lungs to perform activities that usually make you winded, like walking upstairs. When I was training for the races, I did a program that alternated between walking and running. Gradually over time, I was running more than I was walking. Before beginning any exercise-type activities, please consult your doctor, preferably a pulmonologist or allergist-immunologist.

SAVED BY R&B CROONER

Ever since my asthma has been very well controlled, I rarely ever get sick. But if I get ill, it will occur during the change of seasons to spring or fall. One year, I got sick and was down for about four days. I didn't go anywhere but from my bed to the couch. My clients, Zzaje and Marshall Knights, had a gig at a club close to my place, and they were opening for R&B singer Jon B. I said, "God, please don't let this illness make me miss my opportunity to meet him."

By Friday, I felt like I could save my energy all day, and that evening I would be okay to take an Uber a few miles to the venue. I got there and met Jon and his team. They were great! When it was showtime, my clients went on stage. I went to sit with the audience to watch them. Then something happened. I started coughing and I couldn't stop, and there were no seats to be found. It was standing room only.

I went back to the green room. Jon was in there waiting to go on, and he asked, "What are you doing down here?" I told him I had this coughing spell and then I started feeling like I was going to faint and there were no seats. He told me to "have a seat." He saw me with my inhaler in hand and said that he had a family member that has asthma like me. He then informed me that I needed some water. He went to get me something to drink. I stopped coughing and gained my strength but not before my clients came off stage. They were perplexed and wondered why I was back there. I told them what happened and they thanked Jon for helping me out.

Many people can't say an R&B singer, one whose CDs that they own, saved their life. Not sure if he will read this book, but I am very thankful to have had him helping me out that night.

RENEE'S REMEDY

Don't be afraid to share your experience. You never know who can help you in the most unlikely way.

INFLUENCER PERKS

I am a blogger and influencer. I have the opportunity to work with great brands that want me to tell my audience about their business. I was so excited that a restaurant that I loved in college wanted bloggers to talk about their new menu. They were paying us as well as providing us with two free meals. This was around Memorial Day weekend, which meant I would be heading back to Michigan to spend the holiday weekend with my parents. I told my mom I was taking her to dinner, and it was on me. I was so excited because I hadn't been to this restaurant since my undergrad at MSU. My mom and I set off for our girls' night out. The menu was healthy, which excited my mom. I ordered grilled vegetables and meat. We had a great night out, went back home, watched TV with my dad, and went to bed. The following day there was this heavy feeling in my head, but I didn't know what was going on.

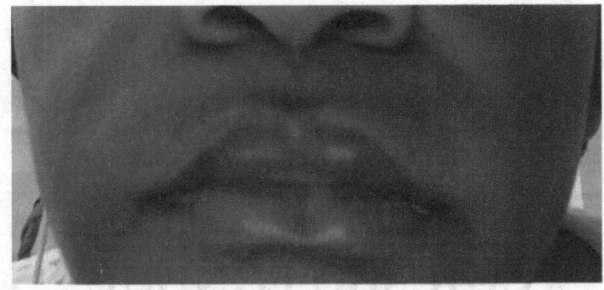

I finally got out of bed and looked in the mirror and to my surprise... Have you seen the movie Hitch starring Will Smith? Well, he had a horrible allergic reaction and his face swelled up something terrible. I saw Hitch in my mirror! I ran downstairs with a hoodie on and said, mom, look at my face. She said I couldn't see anything with that hoodie on. When I removed the hoodie, she gasped! What happened!? I tried to figure out what I did the night before. All I could think of was washing my face before bed. My mom, a few minutes later, said, call the restaurant. This is a delayed reaction to dinner; there had to be nuts in that food.

RENEE'S REMEDY

Everything that looks good to you may not be good for you. Always pay close attention to what you eat and how your body responds.

CHICAGO FONDUE RESTAURANT

There's a chain of fondue restaurants in Chicago. My friend was having a birthday party at one of them. I attended but was sure to tell them about my allergies. They were willing to help in any way possible, even suggesting I get my separate plate, so my food wasn't cooked with their food. Everything worked out, but the only thing we didn't think about was the whole smell of the food, so as it was being prepared, I was near their food steamer with the impact of its contents coming into my face.

The next day I started having asthma symptoms and I wasn't feeling well. I will never again visit a fondue restaurant because even though they gave me my separate fondue pot and different dishes, the steam bath that I was getting from the other people's food contributed to me getting sick.

RENEE'S REMEDY

If you have ever seen a restaurant like this and know that your little one has allergies to the smell of the allergen cooking, please do not go to these restaurants. Much like the ice cream shop, I will not revisit a chain of restaurants. The folks at the fondue restaurant did everything right, but unless I sat at a table by myself, there was no way this would be safe for me.

SISTER'S TRIP

Essence Festival is every Fourth of July weekend in New Orleans, Louisiana. My sister and I have been attending for years, we call it our sister's trip. We live in different states now and these five days allow us to bond, go to concerts and have fun together. Also, the food in New Orleans is amazing, especially for my sister, Chef Alycia Nicole aka Foodieengineer. It's just the easiest time for us to meet on the Fourth of July weekend. She's off work, and we can have a great time and get to see many of our friends. It's wonderful.

My sister, whom I affectionately call Lish for short, can eat everything. I can recall once she wanted to go to a seafood restaurant in New Orleans because she wanted to try a sure crab boil.

We went to Acme, which is exceptionally famous for this dish. I told her I was planning to get a chicken gumbo. I also ordered french fries. My sister was hyper-alert and didn't want anything that was touched with someone's hands. This is said because we noticed many people eating seafood with their hands.

I inquired as to whether the fries were cooked in the same grease as the seafood. I was told that they were. Needless to say, I didn't have those. I ordered the chicken gumbo, which came in the shallowest bowl, so basically, it was about three tablespoons worth of food. My sister was majorly attentive to everything our waiter touched to make sure he wasn't the cause of me getting ill because of any possible errors on his part. I made it out of Acme unscathed, but we stopped at Subway on our way back to the hotel for me to eat dinner.

RENEE'S REMEDY

This is the perfect example of me advocating for myself and my sister being an extra set of eyes to ensure there was no visible cross-contamination. In all honesty, my mom said she didn't want me getting sick to ruin her vacation. I left that restaurant OK because we asked questions and the waiter had answers. All things worked together so that I could order accordingly. Earlier, I mentioned I used to eat at Red Lobster quite regularly without any incident. I eat at restaurants that have seafood on the menu regularly because I know they have taken the proper precautions to prepare my food away from the seafood.

ESSENCE FEST NUTS AT RESTAURANT

I went to the Essence Festival as I do every year and shared accommodations with some girlfriends. One person, I knew for several years, but I didn't know the others. They were friends of my sister, so they didn't know me and did not know about my allergies.

On the first night we went to dinner I reviewed the menu. I am a lover of Brussels sprouts, and they had this on the menu, but the way they were prepared had something to do with nuts. I let the server know that I have a nut allergy. When we received our food, I looked at my plate and I saw green Brussels sprouts. But there was one with a beige light brown small round object sitting in my bowl. Granted, because of my allergies, I can identify unusual things. I don't eat them, but I always ask others about anything I'm uncertain about. I asked the person sitting next to me what she thought the beige light brown object was and she said it resembled a nut to her. I didn't eat anything off the plate, and I quickly called the waitress over. She promptly summoned the server, and I told the gentleman how I specifically said that I was allergic to nuts when I began to place my order, but somehow there's a nut on my plate. He apologized and offered to get me something else. I declined the offer because I was distrustful of anything else that might come my way. As a result, I didn't eat as everyone else dined. Despite this mishap, I had a good time, and so did everyone else.

RENEE'S REMEDY

Sometimes even when you do everything right, something still goes wrong. I should have gone back to the restaurant and explained how they needed to make sure their staff is trained to listen to the customers and look at the dishes before bringing them out. If you do not trust the people making or serving your food, please do not eat.

GETTING RID OF NEGATIVITY

All human beings have all that it takes to be what they want to be even though we have some challenges. Having asthma and allergies was my challenge and since I couldn't change the situation, I learned to live with it. Remember, "never allow a situation you can't change to change or limit you from being what you ought to be." Even at my first funeral, attending an asthmatic patient's funeral and hearing what happened to her scared me. Still, I quickly got rid of negativity, and thanks to my mom for helping me to think this through mentally.

I stick to a particular concept, which is "LIVE LIFE YOU DESERVE." I never let negativity, detractions and excuses make me unable to maximize my potential to the fullest. Still, you need to know that all you need is already within you. Irrespective of what you are facing, you must approach yourself with reverence and love. Self-condemnation and excuses are grievous errors.

I never got jealous of anyone's health or wanted to be someone else. I never deny myself anything. I glue myself to infinity and discover that I don't need to limit myself. I was lucky to have a wonderful family. My parents never raised me to see my asthma as a limitation. They did all they could to make me comfortable, and my sister has always believed that I can do anything even when I am not quite certain I can.

The family has a vital role to play in the life of an asthmatic child. If the family does the necessary teaching and follows the guide, that would make such a child stay positive and won't make a child see a condition as a limitation.

There is nothing you can not do if you only believe and act accordingly. Don't let negativity and what you can't have or can't do cloud your mind. You must lead with positivity and optimism, believe, and work towards the potential that you have from God. Your child has trouble breathing and/or allergies- move past that and look at all the amazing things they can do. It might seem like the odds are against your child, but if you remind them that they have a purpose, and having asthma is not a license to a boring life. As this is being written, I am forty-four years young and all I can say is that I am enjoying my life to the fullest. It doesn't matter that I can't eat everything that everyone else eats. I enjoy what I can eat. I have worked hard to get my lungs healthy where there is nothing I can't do physically. I am blessed to live this life and blessed that my parents didn't put any fear in me around asthma and allergies. Please, as you raise your little ones who have either or both of these diagnoses, remember not to put your fear on them. Hopefully, this book has helped educate you a little more so that you can give your children freedom to explore life.

Prologue

In this next section, I will give you a lot of information about asthma and allergies. I am not your doctor so please make certain you talk with and listen to your doctor about what is best for your child's care. I can tell you that I have never tried any alternative therapy in the treatment of my asthma and allergies, but I know that people are very interested in the information. I am a scientist and I follow science. I have been on a host of medications throughout my life and as mentioned earlier, I am now free of daily medications. I always carry my albuterol inhaler.

The Modern Guide to Navigate Allergies and Asthma

WHAT IS ASTHMA?

Many things seem to come naturally to some people. Maybe you know a girl who's natural at sports. Put her in a uniform and she's off and running. Some people are naturals at playing an instrument; it's like they were born knowing how to count in 4/4 time. Others are naturals at math; give them a test on theorems or equations, and they're happy.

But some people have a problem with something that you'd think would come naturally to everyone. That's breathing. When a person has asthma, it can make breathing very difficult. And when it's hard to breathe, it can affect a person's game, that oboe solo, and even the all-important geometry test.

DEFINITION OF ASTHMA

Asthma is a lung condition that causes a person to have difficulty breathing. Asthma is a common condition. More than six million kids and teens have it.

Asthma affects a person's bronchial tubes, also known as airways. When a person breathes normally, the air is taken in through the nose or mouth and then goes into the trachea (windpipe), passing through the bronchial tubes, into the lungs, and finally back out again. But people with asthma have airways that are inflamed. This means that they swell and produce lots of thick mucus.

They are also overly sensitive or hyperreactive to certain things like exercise, dust, or cigarette smoke. This hyperreactivity causes the smooth muscle that surrounds the airways to tighten up. The combination of airway inflammation and muscle tightening narrows the airways and makes it difficult for air to move through. In most people with asthma, difficulty breathing happens periodically. When it does happen, it is known as an asthma attack which can be counted as an episode or an exacerbation.

ASTHMA ATTACK

A person having an asthma attack may cough, or wheeze (make a whistling sound while breathing), and be short of breath, and feel an intense tightness in the chest. Many people with asthma compare an attack to feeling like a fish with no water. It feels tough to get air in and out of their lungs. An asthma attack can last for several hours or longer if a person doesn't use asthma medication. When an asthma attack is over, the person usually feels better.

Between attacks, a person's breathing can seem completely normal, or a person may continue to have some symptoms such as coughing or, in my case, wheezing. I spent the first ten years of my life wheezing daily. Some people with asthma feel as if they are always short of breath. Other people with the condition may only cough at night or while exercising, and they may never have a noticeable attack.

ORIGIN AND CAUSE

No one knows exactly what causes asthma. It's thought to be a combination of environmental and genetic (hereditary) factors. A teen with asthma may have a parent or other close relative who has asthma or had it as a child. Teens who are overweight may be more likely to have asthma, although a person doesn't have to be overweight to have it.

Asthma symptoms can be brought on by dozens of different things, and what causes asthma flare-ups in one person might not bother another at all.

The things that set off asthma symptoms are called triggers. The following are some of the common triggers:

- **Allergens:** Some people with asthma find that allergens, certain substances that cause an allergic reaction in some people, can be a major trigger. Common allergens are dust mites (microscopic bugs that live in dust), molds, pollen, animal dander, and cockroaches.

- **Airborne Irritants And Pollutants:** Certain substances in the air, such as chalk dust or smoke, can trigger asthma because they irritate the airways. Cigarette smoke is a major cause of asthma symptoms and not just from the asthmatic who smokes. Second hand smoke can trigger asthma symptoms as well. Smoke from someone else's cigarettes. Scented products such as perfumes, cosmetics and cleaning solutions can trigger symptoms, as can strong odors from fresh paint or gasoline fumes. And some research studies have found that high levels of air pollutants such as ozone may irritate the sensitive tissues in the bronchial tubes and can aggravate the symptoms of asthma in some people with the condition.

- **Exercise:** Some people have what's called exercise-induced asthma, which is triggered by physical activity. Although it can be especially frustrating, most cases of exercise-induced asthma can be treated so that people can still enjoy the sports they love.

- **Weather:** Cold or dry air can sometimes trigger asthma symptoms in certain people, as can extreme heat or humidity.

- **Respiratory Tract Infections:** Colds, flu, and other viral infections can trigger asthma in some people.

There are lots of other things that can trigger asthma symptoms For example, a girl's asthma can get worse just before her period. And laughing, crying, and yelling can sometimes cause the airways to tighten in sensitive lungs, triggering an asthma asthma attack. If you knew me as a child then, you know that I laughed myself into more than a few attacks as a child.

DOCTORS DIAGNOSE ASTHMA

Many people with asthma are diagnosed with the condition when they are kids, but some don't find out that they have it until their teens or even later. In diagnosing asthma, a doctor will ask (about any) concerns and symptoms you have, your past health, your family's health, any medications you're taking, any allergies you may have, and other issues. This is called medical history.

The doctor will also perform a physical exam. He or she may recommend that you take some tests. Tests that doctors use to diagnose asthma include spirometry and peak flow meter tests, which involve blowing into devices that measure how well your lungs perform.

Your doctor may also recommend allergy tests to learn if allergies are causing your symptoms or special exercise tests to learn whether your asthma symptoms may be brought on by physical activity. Doctors occasionally use x-rays in diagnosing asthma, but these are usually only to rule out other possible problems. Your family doctor may refer you to a specialist for allergy diagnosis and treatment. Doctors who specialize in the treatment of asthma include those who have been trained in allergy, immunology (how the immune system works), and pulmonology (conditions that affect the lungs).

TREATMENT

There's no cure for asthma, but the condition can usually be managed, and flare-ups can be prevented. Asthma is treated in two ways: by avoiding potential triggers and through the use of medication. Teens who have asthma need to avoid the things that can cause their symptoms. Of course, some things that can cause symptoms can't be completely avoided like catching a cold, but people can control their exposure to some triggers, such as pet dander.

In the case of exercise-induced asthma, the trigger (physical activity) needs to be managed rather than avoided. Exercise can help a person stay healthier overall, and doctors can help athletes find treatments that allow them to participate in sports. Doctors treat every asthma case individually because each person's asthma and the triggers are different. For this reason, doctors have a variety of treatment medications at their disposal. Most asthma medications are inhaled, which means that a person takes the medication by breathing it into the lungs), but asthma medications can also take the form of pills or liquids. They fall into two categories:

1. Relief medications act quickly to halt asthma symptoms once they start. Some medications can be used as needed to stop asthma symptoms (such as wheezing, coughing, and having shortness of breath) when a person first notices them. These medications act fast to control the symptoms, but they are not long-lasting. They are also known as "reliever," "quick relief," or "fast-acting" medications.

2. Controller medications manage asthma and prevent symptoms from occurring in the first place. Many people with asthma need to take medication every day to control the overall condition. Controller medications (also called "preventive" or "maintenance" medications) work differently from rescue medications.

They treat airway inflammation instead of the symptoms (coughing, wheezing, etc.) of asthma. Controller medications are slow-acting and can take days or even weeks to begin working. Although you may not notice them working in the same way as rescue medications, regular use of controller medications should lessen your need for relief medications. Doctors also prescribe controller medications to minimize any permanent lung changes that may be associated with having asthma. Some people with asthma rely only on rescue medications; others use rescue medications and controller medications to keep their asthma in check overall. Each person needs to work closely with a doctor to create an asthma action plan that's right for them.

MONITORING

In addition to avoiding triggers and treating symptoms, people with asthma usually need to monitor their condition to prevent flare-ups and help their doctors adjust medications if necessary. Two of the tools doctors give people to do this are:

1. Peak flow meter. This handheld device measures how well a person can blow out air from the lungs. Your doctor will help decide what your green, yellow and red zones. When I was much younger my green zone was a lot lower than it is today. A peak flow meter reading that falls in the patient's green (or good) zone means the airways are open. Reading in the yellow zone means there's potential for an asthma attack. Reading in the red zone means the asthma attack is severe and could mean that a person needs medication for treatment immediately— maybe even a trip to the doctor or emergency room. People who take daily medicine to control their asthma symptoms, should use a peak flow meter at least one to two times a day and whenever they are having symptoms.

2. Asthma diary. Keeping a journal can also be an effective way to help prevent problems. A daily log of peak flow meter readings, times when symptoms occur, and when medications are taken, can help a doctor develop the most appropriate treatment plan.

ASTHMA STATISTICS

A survey done in 2015-2016 of more than forty thousand adults across the country claims it is one of the first to assess the general population for specific food allergy types and symptoms.

The results show that one in ten adults has a food allergy.

More than half, fifty-one percent, have a severe reaction.

Almost four in ten, thirty-eight percent, report at least one reaction that required emergency care.

But only one in twenty with a convincing food allergy has a doctor-confirmed diagnosis.

And less than a quarter, twenty-four percent, with a food allergy report a current epinephrine prescription.

Research shows that forty-eight percent of the adult population with a convincing food allergy report getting at least one as an adult. They may have had others as a child.

But one out of four adults with a food allergy reported getting their first in adulthood. The study shows that food allergy among adults is a more significant issue in the U.S. than previously thought, particularly the emerging health problem of adults developing their food allergies later in life, even after regularly eating foods that were previously harmless. Researchers also discovered that nearly one in five, or nineteen percent of adults, think they have a food allergy.

ASTHMA IN CHILDREN

WHAT ARE THE SIGNS AND SYMPTOMS?

Common symptoms include coughing (constant or intermittent), wheezing or whistling sounds audible when a child exhales, and shortness of breath or rapid breathing.

Any child who has frequent coughing or respiratory infections (pneumonia or bronchitis) should be evaluated for asthma. The child who coughs after running or crying may have asthma. Recurrent night cough is common, as asthma is often worse at night. Chest tightness and shortness of breath are other symptoms of asthma that may occur alone or in combination with any of the above symptoms. Since these symptoms can occur for reasons other than asthma, other respiratory diseases must always be considered. In a young child, the discomfort of chest tightness may lead to unexplained irritability. They may complain that their chest "hurts" or ``feels funny." Infants who have trouble feeding or who grunt during suckling may have asthma.

HIDDEN ASTHMA

Until rapid breathing, wheezing, and coughing becomes apparent, the condition of many children with asthma will go undetected. These children with asthma usually suffer some degree of airway obstruction, and unless it is controlled the children may suffer respiratory illnesses more frequently than necessary.

Hidden asthma, however, can produce so few recognizable symptoms that even a health care provider might not be able to distinguish abnormal breath sounds with his or her stethoscope, but it may cause subtle problems such as the limitation of physical activity. Pulmonary function testing usually reveals these cases of airway obstruction.

WHAT USUALLY TRIGGERS ASTHMA?

Exercise: Running can trigger an episode in over eighty percent of children with asthma. Bronchodilator medications used before exercise can prevent most of these episodes. When I was training for the races I did I would take a few puffs of my inhaler about ten to twenty minutes before I started running. This helped me to be able to complete the run and not have an asthma attack once the run was over. Without the inhaler it could take me up to an hour to catch my breath. With proper control of asthma, most children with asthma can participate fully in physical activities. There might be exceptions, such as prolonged running, especially during cold weather, allergy season, or illness from a "cold." Swimming seems to be the least asthma-provoking form of exercise. However, there have been recent concerns about excessively chlorinated pools precipitating asthma episodes.

Infections: Respiratory infections, including the flu, frequently trigger severe attack of asthma. Research indicates that these infections are most commonly produced by viruses rather than bacteria. Antibiotics are of no benefit for viral infections and may be of little value in an asthma episode. All children with asthma need to get vaccinated for the flu each year. The American Lung Association's Asthma Clinical Research Centres have shown that the vaccine itself will not precipitate an attack.

Allergy: Many children with asthma have their symptoms triggered by allergies. Allergic children can suffer reactions to ordinarily harmless materials such as pollen, mold, food, or animals.

The allergens involved are common indoor inhalants such as dust mites, feathers, molds, pets, *mice*, insects (especially roaches), outdoor inhalants (molds and pollens), or ingested foods (milk, soy, egg, etc.). Foods are much less frequent causes of asthma. These allergens may produce low-grade reactions, which are of no obvious consequence; however, daily exposure to these allergens may result in a gradual worsening of asthma.

Irritants: Cigarette smoke, air pollution, strong odors, aerosol sprays and paint fumes are some of the substances, which irritate the tissues of the lungs and upper airways. The reaction (cough, wheeze, phlegm, runny nose, watery eyes) produced by these irritants can be identical to those produced by allergens.

Cigarette smoke is an excellent example because it is highly irritating and can trigger asthma. Most people are not allergic to cigarette smoke; that is, there is no known immunologic reaction. Nevertheless, this irritant can be more significant than any allergen. Outdoor air pollution also worsens existing asthma.

Outdoor pollutants known to trigger asthma attacks include ozone, particulate matter, nitrogen dioxide, and sulfur dioxide. Children are already at greater risk from outdoor air pollution than healthy adults. They have smaller air passages that are blocked easier, breathe more rapidly, and are less likely to acknowledge breathing difficulties resulting from pollution and limit their exposure. For a child with asthma, these concerns are especially relevant.

Weather: Children with asthma have cited several climatic conditions as trigger factors. Many identify cold air as triggering asthma. Pulmonary function studies demonstrate that breathing cold air provokes asthma in most children with asthma.

Emotions: A common misbelief is that children with asthma have a significant psychological problem that has caused asthma.

Emotional factors are not the cause of asthma, though emotional stress can infrequently trigger asthma. A child's asthma might only be noticeable after crying, laughing, or yelling in response to an emotional situation. These normal "emotional" responses involve deep rapid breathing, which in turn can trigger asthma, as it does after running.

Emotional stress itself (anxiety, frustration, anger) also can trigger asthma, but the asthmatic condition precedes the emotional stress. Therefore, a child's asthma is not "in his or her head," as many people believe. Emotions are associated with asthma for another reason. Many children with asthma suffer from severe anxiety during an episode due to suffocation produced by asthma. The anxiety and panic can then produce rapid breathing or hyperventilation, which further triggers asthma. During an episode, anxiety and panic should be controlled as much as possible. The parent should remain calm, encourage the child to relax and breathe easily and give appropriate medications.

Treatment should be aimed at controlling asthma. When asthma is controlled, emotional stress will be reduced, and other emotional factors can be dealt with more effectively. Any chronic illness, especially if uncontrolled, can have associated secondary psychological problems. More severe psychological issues require a specialist to help the child and his or her family.

RISK FACTORS FOR DEVELOPING ASTHMA

RISK FACTORS FOR ASTHMA

Anyone with asthma is likely to ask sooner or later, "Why did this have to happen to me?" Answers to questions like this are never simple. However, many pieces of the puzzle are known, and they may help explain why people develop this disease.

Atopy: An Irritating Problem

The immune system is designed to protect your body against harmful bacteria, viruses, and poisons. However, in some people, the immune system will also react violently to some otherwise harmless substances. This problem is known as atopy and can cause several bothersome conditions. Nasal allergies, known as allergic rhinitis, are one of the most common forms of atopy. The nose is overly sensitive to substances in the air, and this leads to hormones in the nasal lining that increase mucous production, itching, and sneezing.

Food allergies are a similar problem, where cells lining the mouth, throat, stomach, skin or intestine react to substances taken in orally. This may cause itching, hives, swelling, vomiting, and in some cases, difficulty breathing or shock. Atopic dermatitis is another troublesome allergic disease. People with atopic dermatitis start developing rashes soon after birth and continue to get them on and off for the rest of their lives. They tend to have very sensitive and dry skin that is easily irritated by various substances.

Asthma is strongly linked to atopy and atopic diseases. Atopic sensitivity causes increased hormone release inside the airways, leading into the lungs when allergens or other substances are inhaled. These hormones cause spasms in the muscles that decrease the size of the airway tubes (airway hypersensitivity). This makes it difficult to get air in and out of the lungs and causes wheezing and shortness of breath.

Atopic diseases frequently occur together. For example, nearly everyone with asthma also has allergic rhinitis. Another common combination is allergic rhinitis, asthma, and a severe allergic reaction to aspirin. The more atopic conditions you have, the more likely you are to develop asthma. These relationships are almost certainly not coincidental and sign that the same problems are causing all these conditions.

Genetics: You Can Pick Your Friends, But Not Your Family

A great deal of asthma appears to be inherited. The disease runs quite strongly in some families, and having a family member with asthma is a major risk factor for developing it yourself. It is believed that this is due to similarities in genes that control the immune system. Your risk for asthma also appears to depend on your ethnic background. For example, African Americans are more likely to develop asthma than other groups. No one is sure why this is true. Theories include particular genes being more common in some parts of the world, as well as differences in exposure to pollution due to social conditions.

Gender: Boys Will Be Boys, And Girls Will Be Girls

Asthma does not practice gender equality. Boys are much more likely to develop asthma than girls, at least until around age twenty. At that point, the risk is more equal, and later in life, asthma becomes more common in women. Why asthma follows this pattern is unknown, but the trends are pretty straightforward.

Premature Birth: Not Ready For Prime Time

Premature birth is a risk factor for developing asthma. People who were born prematurely are significantly more likely to develop asthma. This risk is exceptionally high in people who needed to be on a ventilator early in life, which is common among more premature babies. Having an abnormal environment early in life may lead to unusual sensitivity of the airways, which may become permanent.

Infections: Stop Bugging Me!

There seems to be a relationship between asthma and infections, but it's not a simple one. Many people develop asthma for the first time after a bad cold or pneumonia. It seems like these infections triggered asthma, but the disease keeps going long after the sickness is over.

Scientists think that certain viruses may be particularly likely to cause asthma. However, just catching one of these infections isn't enough to give you asthma. It probably takes having asthma-prone genes, plus a viral infection, plus other factors, to provide you with asthma. So, is living in a spacesuit the best way to keep from getting asthma? Interestingly, people who got more colds as young infants are less likely to get asthma than people who had their first colds later in life. Some scientists believe getting exposed to infections early helps prepare the developing immune system on how to tell the difference between dangerous and harmless.

Air Pollution: Clearing the Air

Air pollution has a significant effect on asthma. Dirty air makes asthma worse, but it also seems to help cause asthma in the first place. People who live in large cities are much more likely to develop asthma, and the dirtier the air, the higher the risk. It's not clear why air pollution makes you prone to asthma, but there's no doubt about the link. In addition to generalized pollution, it is clear that some work-related exposures triggered asthma. Solvents, dust, vapors, and various types of chemicals are common culprits. This disorder is known as occupational asthma.

People with occupational asthma may notice that their symptoms worsen when they go to work or over a workday. Often, they will improve significantly over weekends and vacations and worsen again when they return to work. Avoiding the responsible substance is key to treatment.

Smoking: A Dirty Habit

It shouldn't come as a surprise that smoking increases your risk for asthma. Tobacco smoke contains several hundred chemicals, as well as hot gases and pieces of soot. These have various irritating effects on the airways and may cause airway hyper reactivity even in people who don't have atopy. Being a current smoker roughly quadruples the risk of asthma, and smoking may cause childhood asthma to recur, sometimes after years of having no symptoms.

Unfortunately, tobacco affects the risk of asthma even in people who aren't smokers. Exposure to second-hand smoke (smoke from other people's cigarettes nearby) doubles the risk of developing asthma symptoms Even more significantly, smoking during pregnancy appears to be a significant risk factor for developing asthma. Women who smoke during pregnancy are much more likely to have children who develop asthma. It is believed that the poisonous effects of tobacco smoke cause permanent damage and abnormalities of fetal lungs.

Obesity: A Weight Topic

Your weight affects your risk for asthma. It appears that fatter people are at higher risk for asthma than thinner ones. Some studies suggest that losing weight may improve asthma symptoms as well. No one knows why weight affects asthma, and the relationship was discovered only recently.

Can Your Birth Date Increase Your Risk For Asthma?

Will the time of year when a child is born effect asthma risk?

In this section, we discuss some very recent research that has grabbed media attention: the effect of birth during the time of year on the development of asthma in infants. There has been a well-known association between viral infection (typically from cold viruses and related viruses) in infancy and the risk of developing asthma in childhood. Until now, we haven't known whether early viral infection contributes to the development of asthma or if young kids, who will become asthmatic, just get early viral infections more readily. The current research suggests that viral infection in infancy (less than a year old) contributes to the development of asthma later in childhood.

What Can Be Done

The results from the recent study are both exciting and add significantly to our knowledge about the development of asthma in children. However, we still have much to learn to be able to apply these findings to practice. The main lesson for children at risk of asthma (and for all kids, for that matter) is there's no limit to the risk of getting bronchiolitis. Bronchiolitis is a respiratory viral infection, and like others, peaks in the winter months and is transmitted both by direct contact and from respiratory secretions. It is essential to wash hands well when around other kids who may be sick and be vigilant when in common play areas where there are many kids, especially during the high season.

There isn't much to say about the 'obvious' timing of pregnancy to avoid birth four months before the peak viral season during the winter. It seems that, concerning timing, most pregnancies do not turn out as planned either too quickly or too slowly! This is especially true with the changing demographics of the workforce and couples starting families later in life. If one were so inclined to time a birth during a lower risk period of the year, a couple could begin trying to get pregnant in late winter/early spring. With a few month's leeway, a child would be born early the following year.

Timing pregnancy is like timing the market. It usually doesn't work. The decision to start or grow a family is big enough. Timing that decision based on developing asthma is not worth the worry.

TYPES AND CAUSES OF ASTHMA

Asthma is a disease of the lung that affects the bronchial tubes or airways. The term "asthma" comes from the Greek, meaning "to breathe hard." Medical terminology defines the condition as reversible obstructive airway disease (ROAD). Unlike other conditions that obstruct the airways, such as cystic fibrosis, chronic bronchitis, and emphysema, asthma does not affect sufferers all of the time.

The lungs are a network of airways or bronchial tubes. The bronchial tubes are made of muscles and a mucous membrane. In a healthy lung, air moves freely through the bronchial tubes.

When a asthmatic person has an asthma attack, the membranes inside the bronchial tubes release mucus and become inflamed. The inflammation causes the muscles to contract and create spasms. These muscle spasms are responsible for wheezing. Wheezing is the sound that can be heard as the bronchial tubes constrict, and air tries to escape.

Attacks can vary considerably in their severity and are sometimes relatively mild, but the condition is nevertheless a dangerous one. An asthma attack can quickly spiral out of control at any time. This is particularly true for children.

New Classifications In Types Of Asthma

Although clear patterns do exist, the specific causes of asthma are far from straightforward. Until recently, the condition was divided into two clearly defined types of asthma: extrinsic (allergic) asthma and intrinsic (non-allergic) asthma. Today, asthma is divided into several different types:

- Allergic
- Non-allergic/intrinsic
- Exercise-induced
- Nocturnal
- Occupational
- Steroid-resistant

Allergic Asthma: Ninety percent of all people living with asthma have allergic asthma. Allergic asthma is triggered by allergens—substances capable of causing an allergic reaction.

Causes Of Allergic Asthma: The causes of allergic asthma are wide-ranging. At the top of the list are specific allergens, such as pet dander, pollen, and dust mites. People suffering typical allergen-induced asthma are usually very aware of the offending allergen and try to avoid it.

Pollutants, wood dust, smoke, irritants, chemicals, viral infections, bacteria, stress, emotion, and exercise are other frequently diagnosed causes.

Childhood Allergic Asthma: sthma is the most common chronic condition among children, currently affecting an estimated 6.1 million children under eighteen years. Most childhood asthma is considered an allergic type of asthma. Childhood asthma occurs more often in young boys than girls, and out of all, childhood illnesses account for the most missed days of school.

Research has concluded that maternal smoking can contribute to asthma or other impairment of infant lung function, even before the child is born. Continued exposure to cigarette smoking can irritate the respiratory tract and make infants and children particularly vulnerable to allergic asthma.

Intrinsic Asthma: Asthma is called "intrinsic" when allergies do not play a part. Intrinsic asthma is not likely to develop in children; its typical onset occurs after age forty. Possible causes of intrinsic asthma include respiratory irritants such as perfumes, cleaning agents, fumes, smoke and cold air, upper respiratory infections, and gastroesophageal reflux (GERD). Intrinsic asthma tends to be less responsive to treatment than allergic asthma.

Exercise-Induced Asthma: At least eleven percent of the non-asthmatic population experiences exercise-induced bronchospasm. Many of these people have allergies or a family history of allergies.

Exercise-induced asthma can affect anyone at any age and may be attributed to the loss of heat and moisture in the lungs that occurs with strenuous exercise. Frequent coughing during exercise may be the only symptom of exercise-induced asthma. But in cold, dry conditions, exercise-induced asthma symptoms can be more severe. Some common sense coupled with prophylactic medications for exercise-induced asthma can prevent the onset of asthmatic symptoms for sensitive individuals.

Nocturnal Asthma: Nocturnal, or sleep-related, asthma affects people when they are sleeping and, although termed "nocturnal" (belonging to the night), asthma symptoms can occur regardless of the time of day a person is sleeping. Symptoms of nocturnal asthma tend to be their worst between midnight and 4 a.m. Nocturnal asthma can be triggered by allergens in bedding or the bedroom, decreased room temperature, and gastroesophageal reflux (GERD), among other triggers. An estimated seventy-five percent of asthmatics are affected by nocturnal asthma.

Occupational Asthma: Occupational asthma occurs directly due to breathing chemical fumes, wood dust, or other irritants over long periods of time. An estimated fifteen percent of asthmatics have occupational asthma.

Steroid-Resistant Asthma: In the case of asthma medications, especially steroids, more is not better. Overuse of asthma medications such as reliever medications like albuterol inhalers, can lead to status asthmaticus, a severe asthma attack that doesn't respond to medication and may require mechanical ventilation to reverse. To prevent status asthmaticus, follow your doctor's directions and take medication only as prescribed.

EXERCISE-INDUCED ASTHMA

Everyone needs to exercise, even people with asthma. A robust and healthy body is one of your best defenses against disease. But some people with asthma have "exercise-induced asthma" (EIA). With proper medical prevention and management, you should be able to walk, climb stairs, run, and participate in activities, sports, and exercise without experiencing symptoms. You don't have to let EIA keep you from leading an active life or from achieving your athletic dreams.

What is exercise-induced asthma?

Exercise is a common cause of asthma symptoms. This is usually called exercise-induced asthma (EIA) or exercise-induced bronchospasm (EIB). It is estimated that eighty to ninety percent of all individuals who have allergic asthma will experience symptoms of EIA with vigorous exercise or activity. For teenagers and young adults, this is often the most common cause of asthma symptoms. Fortunately, with better medications, monitoring, and management, you can participate in physical activity and sports and achieve your highest performance level.

What are the symptoms of EIA?

Symptoms of exercise-induced asthma include coughing, wheezing, chest tightness, and shortness of breath. Coughing is the most common symptom of EIA and maybe the only symptom you have. The symptoms of EIA may begin during exercise and will usually be worse five to ten minutes after stopping exercise. Symptoms most often resolve in another twenty to thirty minutes and can range from mild to severe. Occasionally some individuals will experience "late phase" symptoms four to twelve hours after stopping exercise. Late-phase symptoms are often less severe and can take up to twenty-four hours to go away.

What causes EIA?

When you exercise, you breathe faster due to the increased oxygen demands of your body. Usually, during exercise, you inhale through your mouth, causing the air to be dryer and cooler than when you breathe through your nasal passages. This decrease in warmth and humidity are both causes of bronchospasm. Exercise that exposes you to cold air, such as skiing or ice hockey, is more likely to cause symptoms than exercise involving warm and humid air such as swimming. Pollution levels, high pollen counts, and exposure to other irritants such as smoke and strong fumes can also worsen EIA symptoms. A recent cold or asthma episode can cause you to have more difficultly exercising.

How is EIA diagnosed?

It is essential to know the difference between being out of condition and having exercise and asthma. A well-conditioned person will usually only experience the symptoms of EIA with vigorous activity or exercise. To make a diagnosis, your doctor will take a thorough history and perform a series of tests. During these tests, which may include running or a treadmill test, your doctor will measure your lung functions using a spirometer before, during, and after exercise.

Monitoring your peak flows before, during, and after exercise can also help you and your doctor detect narrowing of your airways. Then, using guidelines established by your doctor, you can help prevent asthma symptoms, participate in, and enjoy physical activity. Your doctor will also tell you what to do should a full-blown episode occur.

Treatment and management of EIA

With proper treatment and management, people with EIA can participate safely and achieve their full potential. Proper management requires that you take steps to prevent symptoms and carefully monitor your respiratory status before, during, and after exercise. Taking medication before exercising is vital in avoiding EIA. Proper warm-up for six to ten minutes before periods of exercise or vigorous activity will usually help. Individuals who can tolerate continuous exercise with minimal symptoms may find that proper warm-up may prevent the need for repeated medications.

What types of medications treat/prevent EIA?

There are three types of medications to prevent or treat the symptoms of EIA. Your health care provider can help you determine the best treatment program for you based on your asthma condition and the type of activity or exercise.

The first medication is a short-acting beta2-agonist, also called a bronchodilator. This medication can prevent symptoms and should be taken ten to fifteen minutes before exercise. It will help prevent symptoms for up to four hours. This same medication can also be used to treat and reverse the symptoms of EIA should they occur.

The second medication is a long-acting bronchodilator. It needs to be taken thirty to sixty minutes before activity and only one within a twelve-hour period. Salmeterol can prevent EIA symptoms for ten to twelve hours. This medication should only be used to avoid symptoms and should never be used to relieve symptoms once they occur because it does not offer any quick relief.

The third type of medication is cromolyn or nedocromil. They also need to be taken fifteen to twenty minutes before exercise. There is also some evidence that taking these medications will also help to prevent the late phase reaction of EIA that is experienced by some individuals. These medications should only be used as a preventive measure because they do not relieve symptoms once they begin. Some individuals use one of these medications in combination with a short-acting bronchodilator.

If you have frequent symptoms with usual activity or exercise, talk to your doctor. An increase in your long-term control medications may help. Long-term anti-inflammatory medications such as inhaled steroids can reduce the frequency and severity of EIA.

Teachers and coaches should be informed if a child has exercise-induced asthma. They should be told that the child should participate in activities but require medication before activity. Athletes should also disclose their medications and adhere to standards set by the U.S. Olympic Committee.

What types of sports are best for people with EIA?

Activities that involve only short bursts of exercise or intermittent periods of activity are usually better tolerated. Such sports include walking, volleyball, basketball, and gymnastics, or baseball. Swimming that involves breathing warm and moist air is often well taken. Aerobic sports such as distance running, soccer, or basketball are more likely to cause symptoms. In addition, cold air sports such as ice hockey or ice skating may not be tolerated as well.

NOCTURNAL ASTHMA

Nocturnal asthma. Many parents know all too well the coughing, choking, wheezing and congestion that can keep their children—and the rest of the family—awake at night. "When my three-year-old's asthma acts up, it disrupts his sleep and mine," says Allergy and Asthma Network Mothers of Asthmatics (AANMA) member Rachel Gerke. "I know it is bothering him when he is restless at night, crying or moaning and hitting the sides of the bed when rolling. And when I go in to listen to him, he is either breathing faster, usually from his belly, his chest not rising, or I hear a whistle at the end of his breaths." Rachel's family is not alone. More than twenty million Americans are affected by nocturnal asthma, also called nighttime or sleep-related asthma.

The condition has been reported in medical literature for centuries. Allergy and Asthma Network Mothers of Asthmatics consulted sleep experts—including parents—for advice to help you and your family get a good night's sleep.

Why We're Losing Sleep

When you breathe in, the lungs transport oxygen into the bloodstream, where it's carried to the rest of the body. When you breathe out, they transport the waste product—carbon dioxide—out of the bloodstream. How well these process works varies throughout the day as part of the body's natural circadian rhythm, an internal clock that regulates body mechanics over a twenty-four-hour period. Lungs work best during the day, with peak lung function at about 4 p.m. Several studies show that twelve hours later—around 4 a.m.—lung function is at its lowest. The fluctuation is usually less than ten percent. However, people with asthma can have up to a fifty percent difference between daytime and nighttime lung function.

Gastroesophageal reflux (often called acid reflux or reflux) is a back-wash of stomach acid into the esophagus. It is also a contributing factor to sleep disturbance. AANMA member Carol O'Leary found reflux to be the cause of her son's sleep problems. "After two and a half years of sleepless nights, my son's acid reflux was finally diagnosed and treated. An effective treatment plan helped our whole family start sleeping better," she said. Researchers aren't sure exactly how reflux and asthma interact, but they do see a connection. Adult studies suggest as many as seventy-five percent of adults with asthma also have reflux. Reflux can set off asthma symptoms. Because reflux is more common when a person is lying down, people with asthma may have more difficulty during sleep.

Another sleep-related condition that can worsen nighttime asthma is sleep apnea. This sleep disorder causes repeated pauses in breathing throughout the night. This is a severe problem in itself, but also one that can set off or worsen asthma symptoms. A recent study by the Cincinnati Children's Hospital Medical Center showed that women with asthma are twice as likely to have sleep apnea symptoms as women without asthma. "Please don't rule out sleep apnea as a cause of poor sleep—even in children!" said AANMA member Laurie Soares. "My ten-year-old son has asthma and allergies. He snored, was a mouth breather at night, was tired a lot, and had poor height and weight growth. His father has sleep apnea, so with all those factors present, we had my son's tonsils and adenoids removed. Since then, he sleeps quietly, is gaining weight, and reports that he now has dreams!"

Allergens like pollen or mold that cause allergic reactions can also play a role in sleep problems. Exposure to allergens during the day may set off a chain reaction in the immune system that produces symptoms hours later, as can allergens in the bedroom like dust mites or animal dander. Studies show that postnasal drip and congestion from allergies can cause multiple nighttime "micro-arousals." These awakenings are so brief that the sleeper doesn't even remember them, but they affect alertness the following day.

The Next Day

The effects of nighttime asthma and allergy symptoms reach beyond the bedroom. Children with night time asthma miss more time from school and their parents more time from work than healthy children. School and work performance can suffer when the family can't sleep. Children whose rest is disturbed by asthma symptoms have a higher incidence of psychological problems and poor school performance. Studies show that these children score lower on memory and time-limited tests. The most apparent signs that asthma is disturbing someone's sleep are fatigue, irritability, and reduced alertness the following day. According to Dr. Meltzer, other signs to look for include morning headaches, depression, and impaired concentration.

Doctors use the term "allergic fatigue" to describe the tiredness and general lack of energy experienced by people with nasal allergies. This condition is often blamed on antihistamine medications, many of which causes sedation. But recent studies show that, in addition to other factors, poor sleep quality contributes to the exhaustion people with allergies may feel all day long.

Clean Sleep

Eliminating allergens and potential asthma triggers in the bedroom can make a big difference in your sleep quality. Allergy testing, combined with your symptom history, will help your doctor determine which specific allergens trigger your asthma or allergy symptoms. Then you can focus your efforts on eliminating exposure to those particular allergens.

AANMA member Rachel Clarke reported, "We were amazed at the huge difference in our children's quality of sleep once we removed our carpeting and installed wooden floors. It was expensive but well worth it."

Jan Frey concurred. After finding out her son was allergic to dust mites and mold, she said, "We ripped out carpeting, removed drapes, and stuffed animals and got rid of the clutter that collects dust. We allergy-proofed not only his bed but also his brother's bed in the same room and our bed. We were amazed at the immediate improvement. His nightly wheezing and asthma flare-ups cleared, and he now sleeps more deeply and soundly."

Christine Noriega took a multi-step approach to help her son get a good night's sleep. She said the following: "My son's eczema would flare up and keep him scratching all night, and his asthma would get worse. First, we found out he had food allergies and eliminated those foods. This helped calm his eczema. We also found he was allergic to dust mites. We put dust mite covers on his mattress and pillows, washed his bedding frequently in hot water and put a HEPA filter in his room. When he comes in after playing outdoors, we get him into the bath right away to get rid of the pollen and other allergens. Then we rub Vaseline all over his body and put on cotton pajamas. This helps his eczema. All of these steps are helping calm his asthma, and he's finally getting a good night's sleep."

If cleaning up the bedroom isn't enough to curb allergy symptoms, work with an allergist on treatment options, including immunotherapy (allergy shots), oral and nasal antihistamines, and nasal corticosteroids. Children twelve and older can also be tested to see if they qualify for a medication that reduces the number of antibodies responsible for allergic reactions.

Ensuring Sleep

If you think you are having trouble sleeping due to asthma or allergies, monitor your symptoms, report any problems to your parents or doctor, and keep a sleep journal. This can be part of your daily symptom diary. Talk to your doctor about night time problems. "We need to control asthma both during the day and at night to maximize a patient's health-related quality of life," emphasized Dr. Meltzer. If you notice excessive napping or drowsiness, school problems, hyperactivity, or distractibility, ask your doctor to assess your nighttime symptoms. Talk about your sleep schedule, sleep environment, sleep-related signs, and behavioral issues. You should also carefully monitor your use of medication: Are you taking all doses on time? Adept at using a metered-dose inhaler or nebulizer? Check your inhaler technique at the next medical appointment and talk to the doctor about other medical conditions—like reflux and sleep apnea—that could be contributing to sleep problems.

Rachel Gerke said, "It has taken us all three years of his life, but we've finally started to get my son's asthma symptoms under control." Rachel makes regular appointments for her son with his allergist and asthma program coordinator. "He's had fewer asthma symptoms now that we fine-tuned his medication plan, put wood flooring in his room, removed all stuffed animals, started washing his bedding frequently, and put dust mite-proof covers on his mattress and pillowcases," she explained. "I also think that it made a difference to take the diaper wipes warmer out of his room. It gave off a scent from the wipes that I believe irritated his airways. It is all those little things that a lot of people don't think about doing in their sleeping environment that make a world of difference."

Asthma and allergies don't have to keep you from getting the sleep you need. Work with your medical care team to determine what's causing sleep problems and how you can solve them.

What's On Your Bed?

With all the mattress and pillow options available today, are some better than others for people with asthma and allergies? It depends on what's causing your sneezing and wheezing.

If you have dust mite allergy, the keys to a good night's sleep are using mattress and pillow encasements and monitoring humidity levels. Dust mites need two things to thrive: water, which they absorb from the air and food, and also which they get from you in the form of dead skin cells. Keeping your bedroom's humidity below fifty percent will deprive dust mites of their water source, and a unique cover over your mattress and pillow will deprive them of food. The mattress and pillow encasements will also protect you from allergens in mite body parts and poop.

OCCUPATIONAL ASTHMA

What is occupational asthma?

Asthma is a respiratory disease. It creates a narrowing of the air passages that results in difficulty breathing, tightness of the chest, coughing, and breath sounds such as wheezing.

Occupational asthma refers to asthma that is caused by breathing in specific agents in the workplace. An abnormal response of the body to the presence of an agent in the workplace causes occupational asthma.

The abnormal response, called "sensitization," develops after variable periods of workplace exposure to certain dust, fumes, or vapors. This sensitization may not show any symptoms of disease, or it may be associated with skin rashes (urticaria), hay fever-like symptoms, or a combination of these symptoms.

How does asthma develop?

Asthma is triggered in several ways, and most of them are not entirely understood. For simplicity, we categorize them into two groups: allergic and non-allergic.

Allergic Asthma: Allergic asthma involves the body's immune system. This is a complex defense system that protects the body from harm caused by foreign substances or microbes. Among the essential elements of the defense mechanism are special proteins called antibodies. These are produced when the human body contacts an alien substance or microbe. Antibodies react with substances or microbes to destroy them. Antibodies are often very selective, acting only on one particular substance or type of microbe.

But antibodies can also respond in a wrong way and cause allergic disorders such as asthma. After a period of exposure to an industrial substance, either natural or synthetic, a worker may start producing too many of the antibodies called immunoglobulin E (IgE). These antibodies attach to specific cells in the lung in a process known as "sensitization." When re-exposure occurs, the lung cells with attached IgE antibodies react with the substance. This reaction results in the release of chemicals such as leukotrienes that are made in the body. Leukotrienes provoke the contraction of some muscles in the airways. This causes the narrowing of air passages which is characteristic of asthma.

Non-Allergic Asthma: Following repeated exposure to an industrial chemical, substances such as leukotrienes are released in the lungs. Again, the leukotriene causes narrowing of air passages typical of asthma. The reasons for such release are still not clear because no antibody reaction seems to be involved.

Other Types Of Asthma: In certain circumstances, asthma symptoms may develop suddenly (within twenty-four hours) following exposure to high airborne concentrations of respiratory irritants such as chlorine. This condition is known as reactive airways dysfunction syndrome (RADS). The symptoms may persist for months or years when the sensitized person is re-exposed to irritants. RADS is controversial because of its rarity and the lack of good information on how the lungs are affected and the range of substances that cause it.

How long does asthma take to develop?

There is no fixed period in which asthma can develop. Asthma is a disease that may develop from a few weeks to many years after the initial exposure. Studies carried out on some platinum refinery workers show that in most cases, asthma develops in six to twelve months. But it may occur within ten days or be delayed for as long as twenty-five years. Analysis of the respiratory responses of sensitized workers has established three basic patterns of asthmatic attacks, as follows:

Immediate: Typically develops within minutes of exposure and is at its worst after approximately twenty minutes; recovery takes about two hours.

Late: Can occur in different forms. It usually starts several hours after exposure and is at its worst after about four to eight hours, with recovery within twenty-four hours. However, it can start one hour after exposure with recovery in three to four hours. In some cases, it may start at night, with a tendency to recur simultaneously for a few nights following a single exposure.

Dual Or Combined: This is the occurrence of both immediate and late types of asthma.

How common is asthma?

The frequency of occupational asthma is unknown, although various estimates are available. In Japan, fifteen percent of asthma in males is believed to be occupational. In the United States, two percent of all cases of asthma are thought to be of occupational origin. The number of cases of occupational asthma varies from country to country and from industry to industry. About six percent of animal handlers develop asthma due to animal hair or dust. Between ten and forty-five percent of workers who process subtilisins, the "proteolytic enzymes" like Bacillus subtilis in the detergent industry develop asthma. However, preparations of the enzymes in granulated form, which is less readily inhaled, have reduced the likelihood of asthma.

Approximately five percent of workers exposed to such chemicals as isocyanates and certain wood dust develop asthma.

What factors increase the chances of developing asthma?

Some workplace conditions seem to increase the likelihood that workers will develop asthma, but their importance is not fully known. Factors such as the properties of the chemicals and the amount and duration of exposure are important. However, because only a fraction of exposed workers is affected, factors unique to individual workers can also be important. Such factors include the ability of some people to produce abnormal amounts of IgE antibodies. The contribution of cigarette smoking to asthma is not known. But smokers are more likely than nonsmokers to develop respiratory problems in general.

How does the doctor know if a worker has asthma?

Sufferers from occupational asthma experience difficulty breathing, chest tightness, coughing, and breath sounds such as wheezing, associated with airflow obstruction. Such symptoms should raise the suspicion of asthma. Typically these symptoms are worse on working days, often awakening the patient at night and improving when the person is away from work. While off work, sufferers from occupational asthma may still have chest symptoms when exposed to airway irritants such as dust, or fumes, or upon exercise. Itchy and watery eyes, sneezing, stuffy and runny nose, and skin rashes are other symptoms often associated with asthma.

Lung function tests and skin tests can help to confirm the disease. But some patients with occupational asthma may have normal lung function as well as negative skin tests. The diagnosis of work-related asthma needs to be confirmed objectively.

This can be done by carrying out pulmonary function tests at work and off work. Specific inhalation challenges can demonstrate the occupational origin of asthma and identify the agents responsible when the cause is uncertain. Specific inhalation challenge tests require breathing in small quantities of industrial agents that may induce an asthma attack. These kinds of tests should always be done by specialists trained to do inhalation challenges.

How can we control occupational asthma?

Although there are drugs that may control the symptoms of asthma, it is important to stop exposure. If the exposure to the causal agent is not stopped, treatment will be needed continuously, and the breathing problems may become permanent. People may continue to suffer from occupational asthma even after removal from exposure. For example, a follow-up study of seventy-five patients with asthma caused by red cedar dust showed that only half the patients recovered. The remaining half continued to have asthmatic attacks for a period of one to nine years after the termination of exposure.

Dust masks and respirators can help to control workplace exposure. However, to be effective, these protective devices must be carefully selected, properly fitted, and well maintained. Preventing further exposure might involve a change of job. if a job change is not feasible, relocation to another area of the plant with no exposure may be essential.

HOW TO TELL IF YOU HAVE ASTHMA

Have you, or someone you know, been diagnosed with asthma? If so, you probably have lots of questions.

You may wonder, for example, just what asthma is. The medical definition of asthma is simple, but the condition itself is quite complex. Doctors define asthma as a "chronic inflammatory disease of the airway" that causes the following symptoms:

- Chronic (regular) cough
- Shortness of breath
- Wheezing
- A feeling of tightness in the chest

If you suspect you might have asthma, your doctor will evaluate your medical history and your family, and also perform lung-function tests. Additionally, he or she may prescribe medications that can conclusively determine whether or not you have asthma.

Being Diagnosed—Knowing For Sure If You've Got Asthma

Symptoms of asthma come and go; you may experience some and yet, not know for certain whether you've got asthma or not. For example, you might experience trouble breathing with exercise or get more 'chest' infections than other people do. A persistent cough is a common sign of lung disease. Coughing is a major feature of asthma, especially in children. If your infant or child coughs to the point of vomiting, discuss the possibility of asthma with your doctor. There are reasons other than asthma for a long-term cough, like whooping cough and postnasal drip.

It is important to talk to your doctor about all of your concerns and to ask lots of questions. Something that you may not think is relevant may be useful in pinpointing the problem.

Depending on your circumstances, your doctor will check some or all of the following:

- Your medical history;
- Your family history;
- What are your symptoms;
- How frequently the symptoms occur;
- Whether the symptoms improve with medication;
- Whether you have allergies;
- What are your triggers (that is, what things or situations tend to lead to your experiencing asthma symptoms); or
- Your lung function, using tests like peak flow monitoring and spirometry to determine how quickly you can expel air.

Associated Conditions

Asthma And Allergies: Many people with asthma also have allergies, and your doctor may refer you to an allergist if you're experiencing asthma symptoms. However, just as not everyone who has allergies develops asthma, not everyone who has asthma has allergies. Researchers are still trying to determine the exact relationship between the two.

There is some evidence that allergic sensitivity can start in the womb. If both your parents have allergies, you will have a seventy-five percent chance of also developing them.

Asthma and allergies are related, but they are not the same thing. An allergy is a reaction to a substance that is usually harmless. These substances (allergens) can be inhaled, injected, swallowed, or touched. Being exposed to an allergen may irritate and swell in specific areas of the body, such as the nose, eyes, lungs, and skin. Allergens like pollen, mold, animal dander, and dust mites can make asthma symptoms worse by increasing the inflammation in the airways and making them more sensitive. The best way to find out if you are allergic to something is to have an allergy assessment.

Rhinitis And Sinusitis: Rhinitis and sinusitis are different but related conditions that often make asthma symptoms worse. Rhinitis is when the lining of the nose becomes inflamed, and it usually occurs after exposure to an aero-allergen such as ragweed. Sinusitis is when the lining of the sinus cavities become inflamed and infected, and this generally happens after a viral, bacterial, or fungal infection.

If you have asthma and also develop rhinitis or sinusitis, your doctor may recommend nasal corticosteroid sprays or other treatments in addition to your regular asthma medication. By managing your sinusitis or rhinitis, your asthma may be better controlled.

Gastroesophageal Reflux Disease (GERD): GERD is short for gastroesophageal reflux disease or acid reflux. In most people, GERD is simply ordinary heartburn. Acid reflux can cause asthma symptoms, particularly coughing, when stomach acid travels up the esophagus and irritates the airways of the lungs.

If you do not respond to conventional asthma treatments, or if your asthma symptoms appear to be associated with heartburn, ask your doctor to have you checked for acid reflux.

HOW YOUR DOCTOR DIAGNOSES ASTHMA

How Is Asthma Diagnosed?

Your primary care doctor will diagnose asthma based on your medical history, a physical exam, and results from tests. He or she also will figure out what your level of asthma severity is—that is, whether it's intermittent, mild, moderate, or severe. Your severity level will determine what treatment you will start on.

Medical History

Your doctor may ask about your family history of asthma and allergies. He or she also may ask whether you have asthma symptoms and when and how often they occur. Let your doctor know if your symptoms seem to happen only during certain times of the year or in certain places or if they get worse at night.

Your doctor also may want to know what factors seem to set off your symptoms or worsen them. Your doctor may ask you about related health conditions that can interfere with asthma management. These conditions include a runny nose, sinus infections, reflux disease, psychological stress, and sleep apnea.

Physical Exam

Your doctor will listen to your breathing and look for signs of asthma or allergies. These signs include wheezing, a runny nose or swollen nasal passages, and allergic skin conditions such as eczema. Keep in mind that you can still have asthma even if you don't have these signs on the day that your doctor examines you.

Diagnostic Tests

Lung Function Test: Your doctor will use a spirometry test to check how your lungs are working. This test measures how much air you can breathe in and out. It also measures how fast you can blow air out. Your doctor also may give you medicines and then test you again to see whether the results have improved. If the starting results are lower than normal and improve with the medicine, and if your medical history shows a pattern of asthma symptoms, your diagnosis will likely be asthma.

Other Tests: Your doctor may order other tests if he or she needs more information to make a diagnosis. Other tests may include the following:

- Allergy testing to find out which allergens affect you if any.

- A test to measure how sensitive your airways are. This is called a bronchoprovocation test. Using spirometry, this test repeatedly measures your lung function during physical activity or after you receive increasing doses of cold air or a special chemical to breathe in.

- A test shows whether you have another disease with the same symptoms as asthma, such as reflux disease, vocal cord dysfunction, or sleep apnea.

- A chest x-ray or an EKG (electrocardiogram). These tests will help find out whether a foreign object or other diseases may be causing your symptoms.

Diagnosing Asthma In Young Children

Most children who have asthma develop their first symptoms before five years of age. However, asthma in young children (aged zero to five years) can be hard to diagnose. Sometimes it can be difficult to tell whether a child has asthma or another childhood condition because the symptoms of both conditions can be similar.

Also, many young children who have wheezing episodes when they get colds or respiratory infections don't go on to have asthma after they're six years old. These symptoms may be due to the fact that infants have smaller airways that can narrow even further when they get a cold or respiratory infection. The airways grow as a child grows older, so wheezing no longer occurs when the child gets a cold. A young child who has frequent wheezing with colds or respiratory infections is more likely to have asthma if:

- One or both parents have asthma;
- The child has signs of allergies, including the allergic skin condition eczema;
- The child has allergic reactions to pollens or other airborne allergens; or
- The child wheezes even when he or she doesn't have a cold or other infection.

A lung function test along with a medical history and physical exam is the the most certain way to diagnose asthma. However, this test is hard to do in children younger than five years. Thus, doctors must rely on children's medical histories, signs and symptoms, and physical exams to make a diagnosis. Doctors also may use a four to six-week trial of asthma medicines to see how well a child responds.

Asthma classification

Based on the results of a visit with an asthma specialist, asthma can be classified in these categories, based on National Heart Blood and Lung Institute guidelines.

Mild Intermittent Asthma

- Symptoms of cough, wheeze, chest tightness, or difficulty breathing less than twice a week
- Asthma attacks—brief, but the intensity may vary
- Nighttime symptoms less than twice a month
- No symptoms between asthma attacks
- Lung function test FEV1 [forced expiratory volume, one second] equal to or above eighty percent of normal values
- Peak flow less than twenty percent variability AM-to-AM or AM-to-PM, day-to-day

Mild Persistent Asthma

- Symptoms of cough, wheeze, chest tightness, or difficulty breathing three to six times a week
- asthma attacks-may affect the activity level
- Nighttime symptoms three to four times a month
- Lung function test FEV1 equal to or above eighty percent of normal values
- Peak flow less than twenty to thirty percent variability

Moderate Persistent Asthma

- Symptoms of cough, wheeze, chest tightness, or difficulty breathing daily
- Asthma attacks-may affect the activity level
- Nighttime symptoms five or more times a month
- Lung function test FEV1 above sixty percent but below eighty percent of normal values
- Peak flow more than thirty percent variability

Severe Persistent Asthma

- Continuous Symptoms of cough, wheeze, chest tightness, or difficulty breathing

- Nighttime symptoms frequently
- Lung function test FEV1 less than or equal to sixty percent of normal values
- Peak flow more than thirty percent variability. The level of asthma severity will determine what types of medicine you will need to get your asthma under control.

WHAT DOES A PULMONOLOGIST DO?

Pulmonary Function Tests

Pulmonary function tests are a group of tests that measure how well the lungs take in and release air and how well they move oxygen into the blood.

How The Test Is Performed

In a spirometry test, you breathe into a mouthpiece connected to an instrument called a spirometer. The spirometer records the amount and the rate of air that you breathe in and out over a period of time.

For some of the test measurements, you can breathe normally and quietly. Other tests require forced inhalation or exhalation after a deep breath. Lung volume measurement can be done in two ways:

The most accurate way is to sit in a sealed, clear box that looks like a telephone booth (body plethysmograph) while breathing in and out into a mouthpiece. Changes in pressure inside the box help determine the lung volume.

Lung volume can also be measured when you breathe nitrogen or helium gas through a tube for a certain period. The concentration of the gas in a chamber attached to the tube is measured to estimate the lung volume.

To measure diffusion capacity, you breathe a harmless gas for a very short time, often one breath. The concentration of the gas in the air you breathe out then is measured. The difference in the amount of gas inhaled and exhaled can help estimate how quickly gas can travel from the lungs into the blood.

How To Prepare For The Test

Do not eat a heavy meal before the test. Do not smoke for four to six hours before the test. You'll get specific instructions if you need to stop using bronchodilators or inhaler medications. You may have to breathe in medication before the test.

How The Test Will Feel

Since the test involves some forced breathing and rapid breathing, you may have some temporary shortness of breath or light-headedness. You breathe through a tight-fitting mouthpiece, and you may be wear nose clips.

Why The Test Is Performed

Spirometry measures airflow. By measuring how much air you exhale and how quickly, spirometry can evaluate a broad range of lung diseases. Lung volume measures the amount of air in the lungs without forcibly blowing out. Some lung diseases such as emphysema and chronic bronchitis can make the lungs contain too much air. Other lung diseases such as fibrosis of the lungs and asbestosis make the lungs scarred and smaller so that they contain too little air.

Testing the diffusion capacity, also called the DLCO, allows the doctor to estimate how well the lungs move oxygen from the air into the bloodstream.

Normal Results

Normal values are based on your age, height, ethnicity, and sex. Normal results are expressed as percentages. A value is usually considered abnormal if it is less than eighty percent of your predicted value.

Normal value ranges may vary slightly among different laboratories. Talk to your doctor about the meaning of your specific test results.

What Abnormal Results Mean

Abnormal results usually mean that you may have some chest or lung disease.

Risks

The risk is minimal for most people. There is a very small risk of partially collapsed lung in people with a certain type of lung disease. The test should not be given to a person who has experienced a recent heart attack, or who has certain other types of heart disease.

Consideration

Your cooperation while performing the test is crucial to get accurate results. A poor seal around the mouthpiece of the spirometer can give poor results that can't be interpreted. Do not smoke before the test.

Pulmonary Function Tests (PFTs)

Pulmonary function tests (PFTs) are a series of different breathing tests led by a trained pulmonary function technologist, usually done at a hospital or clinic. Some national standards and guidelines help make sure that everyone does and interprets pulmonary function tests in the same way.

To learn about your lung health, your doctor may want you to have several pulmonary function tests done, including spirometry, lung volumes, diffusing capacity, and arterial blood gases. Most of these breathing tests are done by blowing into a tube while sitting in a chair.

Before you have pulmonary function tests, you may get specific instructions on how to get ready for the tests, such as the following:

- Wear loose clothing that will not restrict your ability to breathe deeply.

- Avoid large meals prior to your test time which will make it more comfortable for you to breathe deeply.

- Don't use your inhalers on the day of the test, if possible. At your appointment, the equipment will be set up for you after being cleaned and disinfected, including a clean mouthpiece.

- Allow the technologist to tell you what to do before each test. Listen carefully and follow the coaching from the technologist. If you don't understand what to do, ask him or her to tell you differently.

Spirometry

Spirometry is a very common test to help you and your doctor understand your asthma better, and check how it is improving with treatment. The National Heart, Lung, and Blood Institute (NHLBI) guidelines recommend that all persons with asthma have spirometry done at the beginning of care, again as treatments are started, and at least every year for continuing care. Spirometry measures how much air you can inhale (breathe in) and exhale (breath out), as well as how fast you can exhale. For this test, you may be asked to breathe quickly, forcefully, or slowly. The test is repeated at least three times and often more to ensure that the test is reliable.

Your doctor may order a bronchodilator to be given as part of spirometry. A bronchodilator is an inhaled medication that may dilate, or open up, your airways. Spirometry is often done before and after the bronchodilator to show any response to the medicine. Your response may help your doctor find out what kind and how much if any, airway disease you may have and whether you need medication to improve your breathing.

Forced Vital Capacity (FVC)

Forced vital capacity measures the amount of air exhaled from full inspiration to full expiration (empty). You will be asked to breathe in as deeply as you can and immediately blow out as hard and fast as possible until you feel you cannot blow any longer. With the help of a computer, the FVC effort will make a graph called a "flow volume curve" or "flow-volume loop." This graph will look different for everyone. The measurements taken from this test are key in helping your doctor diagnose asthma

Forced Expiratory Volume In The First Second (FEV1): FEV1 measures the amount of air you can forcefully blow out in the first second of the FVC. If this number is lower than what is considered normal, it may mean asthma. The ratio between your FEV1 and FVC, known as FEV1/FVC, can also help diagnose asthma. If your FEV1/FVC is lower than normal, it can mean asthma. It is normal for this number to go down somewhat with age.

Peak Expiratory Flow (PEF) Or Peak Flow (PF): Peak expiratory flow is the fastest flow rate reached at any time during an FVC. This depends a lot on your effort during the test.

Lung Volumes

The doctor may also order tests that measure your lung volumes. There are eight separate volumes of air that can be measured during the lung volumes test. The three most commonly used ways of measuring lung volumes are:

Nitrogen Washout: Done by normal breathing of pure oxygen while exhaled gas is collected and analyzed.

Body Box: Also known as plethysmography, is done while sitting in an enclosed clear chamber while asked to perform a series of very small panting breaths. This is the most accurate way to measure lung volumes.

Helium Dilution: Done by normal breathing of gas mixture of helium and oxygen. People with asthma may show changes in their lung volumes. This can help the doctor diagnose and treat asthma.

Diffusing Capacity (DLCO)

Diffusing capacity of the lungs measures how well gases such as oxygen move from the lungs into the blood. There are several ways to measure this, but the most common way is the ten second single breath-hold technique. Results of this test can tell your doctor about the amount of damage or abnormality present where the air and the blood meet. While this test does not specifically test for asthma, it may help your doctor to diagnose you correctly

Arterial Blood Gases (ABGs)

This is a blood test that may be ordered with your PFTs to give your doctor even more information about your lung health. ABGs can show how well your lungs are getting oxygen into your blood and carbon dioxide out of your blood. For this test, a blood sample is drawn from your artery, in your wrist or elbow area.

What We Can Learn From PFTs

A doctor will look over the results of your PFTs and see how you are doing by comparing them to predicted values normal for a person your age, size, and sex. Height is important because taller people may have bigger lungs. Many things can change the results in PFTs. These include not only the health of your lungs but also the skill of the person testing you, your effort, differences in equipment, and differences in hospital or clinic procedures. A medical diagnosis is not likely to be made from PFTs alone.

Most lung diseases are labeled either as restrictive or obstructive. They are not the names of actual lung diseases, but the labels help group types of lung diseases together. Asthma is an obstructive disease, which means that it causes people to have trouble breathing out.

Words like mild, moderate, or severe may be used to describe how severe the problem is. Ask your doctor to explain the results so that you know what they mean for you. A PFT may be repeated as often as your doctor thinks it is needed. Lung problems can be checked for change by regular pulmonary tests. Check with your insurance company to see how often PFTs are covered for you. The NHLBI guidelines recommend them yearly for people with asthma.

SHOULD I SEE AN ALLERGIST?

Asthma and other allergic diseases are two of the most common health problems. Approximately fifty million Americans have asthma, hay fever, or other allergy-related conditions.

Some allergy problems—such as a mild case of hay fever—may not need any treatment. Sometimes allergies can be controlled with the occasional use of an over-the-counter medication. However, sometimes allergies can interfere with day-to-day activities or decrease the quality of life. Allergies can even be life-threatening.

The Allergist Treats Asthma And Allergies

An allergist is a physician who specializes in the diagnosis and treatment of asthma and other allergic diseases. The allergist is specially trained to identify the factors that trigger asthma or allergies. Allergists help people treat or prevent their allergy problems. After earning a medical degree, the allergist completes a three-year residency-training program in either internal medicine or pediatrics. Next, the allergist completes two or three more years of study in allergy and immunology. You can be certain that your doctor has met these requirements if he or she is certified by the American Board of Allergy and Immunology.

What Is An Allergy?

One of the marvels of the human body is that it can defend itself against harmful invaders such as viruses or bacteria. But sometimes, the defenses are too aggressive, and harmless substances such as dust, molds, or pollen are mistakenly identified as dangerous. The immune system then rallies its defenses, including several chemicals to attack and destroy the supposed enemy. In the process, some unpleasant and, in extreme cases, life-threatening symptoms may be experienced in the allergy-prone individual.

The Cause Of Allergic Reactions

There are hundreds of ordinary substances that can trigger allergic reactions. Among the most common are plant pollens, molds, household dust (dust mites), cockroaches, pets, industrial chemicals, foods, medicines, feathers, and insect stings. These triggers are called "allergens."

Types Of Allergy Problems

An allergic reaction may occur anywhere in the body but usually appears in the nose, eyes, lungs, lining of the stomach, sinuses, throat, and skin. These are places where special immune system cells are stationed to fight off invaders inhaled, swallowed, or come in contact with the skin.

Allergic Rhinitis (Hay Fever): Allergic rhinitis is a general term used to describe the allergic reactions in the nose. Symptoms may include sneezing, congestion, runny nose, itching of the nose, the eyes, and/or the roof of the mouth. When this problem is triggered by pollens or outdoor molds during the spring, summer, or fall, the condition is often called "hay fever." When the problem is year-round, it might be caused by exposure to house dust mites, household pets, indoor molds, or allergens at school or in the workplace.

Asthma: Asthma symptoms occur when airway muscle spasms block the flow of air to the lungs and/or the linings of the bronchial tubes become inflamed. Excess mucus may clog the airways. An asthma attack is characterized by difficult or restricted breathing, a tight feeling in the chest, coughing, and/or wheezing. Sometimes a chronic cough is the only symptom. Asthma trouble can cause only mild discomfort, or it can cause life-threatening attacks in which breathing stops altogether.

Contact Dermatitis/Skin Allergies: Contact dermatitis, eczema, and hives are skin conditions caused by allergens and other irritants. Often the reaction may take hours or days to develop, as in the case of poison ivy. The most common allergic causes of rashes are medicines, insect stings, foods, animals, and chemicals used at home or work. Allergies may be aggravated by emotional stress

Anaphylaxis: Anaphylaxis is a rare, potentially fatal allergic reaction that affects many parts of the body at the same time. The trigger may be an insect sting, a food (such as peanuts), or a medication. Symptoms may include the following:

- Vomiting or diarrhea.
- Dangerous drop in blood pressure.
- Redness of the skin and/or hives.
- Difficulty breathing.
- Swelling of the throat and/or tongue.
- Loss of consciousness.

Often, the symptoms of asthma or allergies develop gradually over time. Allergy sufferers may become used to frequent symptoms such as sneezing, nasal congestion, or wheezing. With the help of an allergist, these symptoms can usually be prevented or controlled with a major improvement in quality of life.

Effectively controlling asthma and allergies requires planning, skill, and patience. The allergist, with his or her specialized training, can develop a treatment plan for your condition. The goal will be to enable you to lead a life that is as normal and symptom-free as possible.

A visit to the allergist might include the following:

Allergy Testing: The allergist will usually perform tests to determine what allergens are involved.

Prevention Education: The most effective approach to treating asthma or allergies is to avoid the factors that trigger the condition in the first place. Even when it is not possible to completely avoid allergens, an allergist can help you decrease exposure to allergens.

Medication Prescriptions: Several new and effective medications are available to treat both asthma and allergies.

Immunotherapy (Allergy Shots): In this treatment, patients are given injections every week or two (given injections once a month after a weekly buildup period) build up period of weekly of some or all of the allergens that cause their allergy problems. Gradually the injections get stronger and stronger. In most cases, allergy problems get less and less over time.

ALLERGY TESTING FOR CHILDREN

What is an allergy?

An allergy is the body's immune system response to specific elements in the environment. Children with allergies react to certain substances in their everyday environment, which usually don't cause reactions in other children.

About twenty percent of Americans—one in every five adults and children—have allergies, including allergic asthma. About eighty percent of children with asthma have allergies. Food allergies occur in eight percent of children younger than age six.

How do allergies affect children, and how do they get them?

Children seem to be more vulnerable to allergies than adults. Allergies to food, house dust mites, animal dander, and pollen are most common. These allergies show up as allergic rhinitis (hay fever), asthma, and atopic dermatitis (eczema). Also, frequent ear infections may be related to allergies.

If both parents have allergies, their (biological) child has a seventy-five percent chance of having allergies. If one parent is allergic, or if relatives on one side of the family have allergies, then the child has about a fifty percent chance of developing allergies.

There is some evidence that breastfeeding helps prevent children from developing food allergies and eczema.

What are the signs or symptoms of allergy in a child?

Symptoms develop as the body releases special antibodies called IgE (immunoglobin E), which are the key players in an allergic reaction. These special antibodies can trigger the release of chemicals that can cause the physical symptoms and changes associated with allergies such as the following:

- Hives
- Runny nose
- Itching or swelling of the lips, tongue, or throat
- Upset stomach, cramps, bloating, or diarrhea
- Wheezing or difficulty breathing
- Anaphylactic shock—a life-threatening body reaction requiring emergency care

What tests are generally used to diagnose allergies?

First, keep in mind that allergy tests are not the sole basis for diagnosing or treating an allergy. Health care providers make an allergy diagnosis based on several factors such as the following:

- History of the patient's experiences and family history of allergy/asthma
- Physical exam of the patient to detect signs of allergy
- Allergy testing for sensitivity to specific allergens

Allergy tests help your physician confirm allergies you may have. When an allergy test pinpoints a reaction to a specific allergen(s), your health care provider also can use this information for recommending steps you can take at home to reduce exposure in addition to developing "immunotherapy"—allergy shots—specifically for you, if appropriate.

Skin Tests For Allergies: Skin prick tests are the most common tests for allergy. Small amounts of suspect allergy triggers are introduced through the skin of the arm or back by pricking or puncturing the skin with a needle or similar device. If you are allergic to a substance, you will see a wheal. A raised red itchy bump is called a "wheal." Reactions usually appear within fifteen minutes. This positive result indicates that the IgE antibody is present when you come in contact with the specific allergen. The wheal size is important: the bigger it is, the more sensitive you are to that particular substance. This test is the least time-consuming and expensive. You may have to discontinue certain medications, especially antihistamines, several days before testing.

Blood Tests For Allergies: The RAST (radioallergosorbent test) and related blood tests use radioactive or enzyme markers to detect levels of IgE antibodies. These tests are useful when a child is very young, skin test is difficult due to a widespread skin rash, anxiety about skin pricks, or if the patient has the potential for a sudden and severe allergic response to test allergens.

Skin tests and these blood tests are very comparable in their ability to diagnose sensitivity to specific allergens. Skin tests are a little more accurate than blood tests and are still considered the "gold standard" for allergy testing.

Elimination Diet: An elimination diet is rarely used now, because it is so difficult to follow. Positive food tests are used to guide restriction of certain foods). The chief drawback to an elimination diet is making sure you eat "pure" foods. Common food allergens are "hidden ingredients" in hundreds of packaged or processed foods.

Are there other allergy tests?

The tests described above are considered the most effective and usual way to help diagnose allergies to specific substances. You also may hear of other allergy tests. These tests may work, but as yet, they are unproven or not universally accepted allergy testing methods. If your health care provider suggests one of these tests, consider getting a second opinion about allergy testing:

- Cytotoxicity blood test
- Electroacupuncture biofeedback
- Urine autoinjection
- Skin titration
- Sublingual provocative testing
- Candidiasis allergy theory
- Basophil histamine release

What kind of doctor does allergy testing?

Allergy testing usually is done by an allergist. An allergist specializes in diagnosing and treating allergies. Some allergists specialize in treating children. The specialty you are looking for is an allergy and immunology doctor. Many of these specialists specialize in asthma and allergies.

TIPS FOR CONTROLLING YOUR ASTHMA

Take Control Of Asthma

New Guidelines from the National Heart, Lung, and Blood Institute (NHLBI)'s National Asthma Education and Prevention Program use the latest research to help you take control of your asthma symptoms and reduce the effects of the disease on your life. Your goal should be to feel good, be active all day and sleep well at night. All patients with asthma should accept nothing less.

If your asthma is in control, you should expect:

- No or few asthma symptoms, even at night or after exercise
- Prevention of all or most asthma attacks
- Participation in all activities, including exercise
- No emergency room visits or hospital stays
- Less need for quick-relief medicines
- No or few side effects from medicines.

Keep Asthma Symptoms In Check

Many of the twenty-two million Americans who have asthma limit their activities and miss work or school. The disease also can kill. Almost four thousand people die from asthma each year, and most of these deaths are preventable. Uncontrolled asthma and asthma deaths happen when the disease is not treated correctly or sometimes because people do not know they have asthma.

Effective asthma treatment begins with the right diagnosis early in the disease. Delays can lead to permanent lung damage.

Your doctor first decides how to treat your asthma by looking at what your symptoms are now and what they have been in the past. The doctor also will try to determine your risk for future attacks. This information will help you and your doctor develops a plan to manage your disease and keep your asthma under control.

If you just started treatment or have frequent symptoms, your doctor may want to see you every two to six weeks. Once treatment is underway, doctor visits every one to six months to check asthma control, even when you have no symptoms.

During your visits, the doctor will review your symptoms, activities, and medicines. Between visits, you need to monitor your asthma by keeping an asthma diary to track your symptoms and using a peak flow meter to measure the airflow from your lungs. With either method, you also should keep track of your medication use. This information will help you and your doctor decide if any changes in your treatment plan are needed.

Avoid Asthma Triggers

Often the best way to control asthma symptoms is to stay away from whatever causes or "triggers" them. Asthma triggers frequently include the following:

- Things to which you are allergic (allergens) such as pollen, dust mites, cockroaches, molds, and animal danders;

- Tobacco smoke, air pollution, formaldehyde, and other volatile organic substances; medicines such as aspirin and acetaminophen;

- Cold air; or

- Exercise.

Some health problems also can trigger or make asthma symptoms worse. These include obesity, obstructive sleep apnea, acid reflux, the common cold, sinus infections, stress, and depression. Let your doctor know if you have one of these conditions so you can discuss the best approach to control both your health problem and your asthma symptoms.

Use Proper Asthma Medication

Today, there are many effective medicines to treat asthma. Most people with asthma need two kinds. Quick-Relief Medicines: These medicines are taken at the first sign of any asthma symptoms for immediate relief:

- Short-acting inhaled beta2-agonists
- Anticholinergics

Your doctor also may recommend you use these medicines before exercise. Quick-relief medicines can stop asthma symptoms, but they do not control airway inflammation that causes the symptoms. If you find that you need your quick-relief medicine to treat asthma symptoms more than twice a week, or two or more nights a month, your asthma is not well controlled. Be sure to tell your doctor.

Long-Term Control Medicines: These medicines are taken every day to prevent symptoms and attacks:

- Antileukotrienes or leukotriene modifiers
- Cromolyn sodium and nedocromil
- Inhaled corticosteroids
- Long-acting inhaled beta2- agonists (never taken alone)
- Methylxanthines
- Oral corticosteroids
- Immunomodulators
- Antimuscarinic agents (Spiriva)

These medicines are taken every day even if you do not have symptoms. The most effective long-term control medicines reduce airway inflammation and help improve asthma control.

Your doctor will work with you to find the right medicine, or combination of medicines, to manage your asthma, and will adjust the type and amount based on your symptoms and control. The goal is to have you feel your best with the least amount of medicine. See an Allergist, an Asthma Specialist. An allergist can help you learn more about your asthma and develop a treatment plan that works for you.

The guidelines say that you should see an asthma specialist if you:

- Have asthma symptoms every day and often at night that cause you to limit your activity;
- Have had a life-threatening asthma attack;
- Do not meet the goals of your asthma treatment after three to six months, or your doctor believes you are not responding to the current treatment;
- Have symptoms that are unusual or hard to diagnose;
- Have conditions such as severe hay fever or sinusitis that complicate your asthma or your diagnosis;
- Need more tests to find out more about your asthma and the causes of your symptoms;
- Need more help and instruction on your treatment plan, medicines, or asthma triggers;
- Might be helped by allergy shots;
- Need oral corticosteroid therapy or high-dose inhaled corticosteroids;
- Have taken oral corticosteroids more than twice in one year;
- Have stayed in a hospital because of your asthma; or
- Need help to identify your asthma triggers.

ASTHMA ATTACKS

What's An Asthma Attack?

For someone with asthma, the airways in the lungs are a problem. They're always a little swollen or irritated, but during an asthma attack, also called an asthma flare-up, attack, episode, or exacerbation), the problems worsen. Sticky mucus clogs these important tubes. And the muscles around the airways tighten up, further narrowing the airway. This leaves very little room inside for the air to flow through. Think of straw with walls that are getting thicker and narrower, leaving less and less space inside for air to get through. An attack can cause coughing, chest tightness, wheezing, and trouble breathing. A person having an attack also might sweat or feel his or her heart beating faster. If the attack is severe, the person may struggle to breathe even while sitting still. He or she may not be able to speak more than few words at a time without pausing for breath.

Because they can be life-threatening, all asthma attacks demand attention. Someone having an asthma attack might need to take rescue medication, visit the doctor, or even go to the hospital. Having a set of instructions called an asthma action plan can help you know which course of action is needed.

Attack Causes

Certain things can bring on symptoms in someone who has asthma. These are known as triggers. It may not always be clear as to what a person's triggers are, but common triggers include tobacco smoke, cold air, exercise, and infections, such as colds.

A lot of people who have asthma also have allergies. In these people, the allergens—the things that cause the allergic symptoms—can also cause asthma attacks.

Examples of common allergic triggers include animal dander, dust mites, mold, and cockroaches. Exposure to a trigger can lead to an asthma flare-up in several ways. It can worsen the swelling in the airways and increase the amount of mucus made there. It can also cause the muscles around the airways to tighten, making the airways even narrower.

Left untreated, a flare-up can last for several hours or even several days. Relief medications often take care of the symptoms pretty quickly, and most people feel better once the asthma attack is over, although it can take several days to completely clear up.

Can You Predict A Flare-Up?

Attacks vary a lot from person to person and even from attack to attack. Some attacks happen suddenly when a person has been exposed to a trigger, such as tobacco smoke. But other attacks happen because problems in the airways have been building up over time, especially in people whose asthma is not well controlled.

Asthma attacks can and should be treated at their earliest stages, so it's important to recognize early warning signs. These are things that a person might experience just before an attack occurs. These clues are unique to each person and maybe the same or different with each asthma attack. Early warning signs include the following:

- Coughing, even if you don't have a cold;
- Throat clearing;

- Rapid or irregular breathing;
- Unusual fatigue;
- Restless sleep; or
- Difficulty with exercise.

A peak flow meter also can be a useful tool in predicting whether an asthma attack is on its way.

Preventing Asthma Attacks

You also have the power to prevent asthma attacks, at least some of the time.

Here's what you can do, regarding the following:

- Have your inhaler and spacer with you always.
- Stay away from triggers that you know may cause asthma attacks.
- Take your controller medicine as directed. Don't skip it or take less of it because you are feeling better.
- Work with your parents and doctor to follow an asthma action plan.

HOW IS ASTHMA TREATED

What's The Difference Between Rescue and Controller Medications?

Asthma medicine comes in two main types: controller medicine and reliever medicine. Reliever medications also called quick-relief or fast-acting medications, work immediately to relieve asthma symptoms when they occur. These types of medicines are often inhaled directly into the lungs, where they open up the airways and relieve symptoms such as wheezing, coughing, and shortness of breath, often within minutes. But as effective as they are, rescue medications don't have a long-term effect. Controller medications, also called preventive or maintenance medications, work overtime to reduce airway inflammation and help prevent asthma symptoms from occurring. They may be inhaled or swallowed as a pill or liquid.

Relief Medications

Quick-acting bronchodilators, usually given through an inhaler or a nebulizer, loosen the tightened muscles around inflamed airways and are the most often prescribed rescue medications. The most common of these are called beta2-agonists. These medications are related to adrenaline and usually, work within minutes to provide temporary relief of symptoms. If the bronchodilator alone doesn't resolve a severe asthma attack, other medications may be given by mouth or injection to help treat it.

If you have been prescribed a relief medication, it's important to keep these medicines on hand. That means at home, at the mall, at sports practice, and even on vacation. Relief medications, although an important part of asthma treatment, can be overused. Talk with your doctor about how often you use the relief medication. If it's too much, the doctor also may prescribe a controlled medicine designed to prevent asthma flare-ups from happening.

Controller Medications

Because your airways may be inflamed even in-between flare-ups, the controller medications may be needed to prevent unexpected asthma flare-ups. Slower-acting controller medicines can take days to weeks to start working, but when they do, they prevent airway inflammation and keep the lungs from making too much mucus.

There are a variety of controller medications, but inhaled corticosteroids are most common. They're usually given through an inhaler or nebulizer. Despite their name, corticosteroids are not the same as performance-enhancing steroids used by athletes. They are a safe and proven form of treatment for asthma.

Inhaled corticosteroids are the preferred long-term treatment for children with frequent asthma symptoms. Research shows that they improve asthma control, and their risk of causing long-term negative effects is minimal. But corticosteroids that are swallowed in liquid or pill form may cause side effects if used daily over a long period.

Long-acting bronchodilators can also be used as controller medications. These relax the airway muscles for up to twelve hours but can't be used for quick relief of symptoms because they don't start to work immediately.

Even if you take controller medicine regularly, rescue medication will still be needed to handle flare-ups when they occur.

Working With The Doctor

Your doctor will determine which type of medicine you need, depending on how frequent and how severe the asthma symptoms are. Both the type and dosage of medication that you need are likely to change, with the goal being to have you on the lowest amount of medication necessary for effective asthma management.

You're an important player in your asthma treatment. For example, you can track how well the medicine is working by using a peak flow meter. You also can record information in an asthma diary and ask your doctor to create an asthma action plan if you don't already have one. By reporting any concerns or changes in your symptoms, you can provide information to help the doctor select the best course of treatment.

Action Plans Are Personalized

Asthma varies from person to person, so there isn't a one-size-fits-all asthma action plan. Each plan will be somewhat different, but a key part of any action plan will detail what you need to do during a flare-up. It will tell you when you need to take your rescue medication, how much to take in different circumstances, and when it's time to call the doctor or go to the emergency department for care.

Many action plans use the "zone system," based on the colors of a traffic light. This is the same color system used on peak flow meters. Action plans use symptoms, peak flow readings, or both to help you determine what zone your asthma is in:

- The green zone, or safety zone, explains how to manage your asthma daily when you're feeling good.
- The yellow zone, or caution zone, explains how to look for signs that your asthma is getting worse.
- It also instructs you on which medications to add to bring your asthma back under control.
- The red zone, or danger zone, explains what to do when a flare-up is severe.

The color system makes it easy to figure out which instructions apply to you based on your peak flow meter reading. Your "personal best" peak flow reading is an important measurement to include on the plan, so you'll have something to compare the new numbers to. In addition to information about flare-ups, your action plan may include the following:

- Emergency phone numbers and locations of emergency care facilities;

- A list of triggers and how to avoid them;

- Steps to take before exercising;

- A list of early asthma attack symptoms to watch for and what to do when they occur; and

- The names and dosages of all your medications and when and how they should be used.

UNDERSTANDING THE DIFFERENT TYPES OF ASTHMA MEDICATIONS

Can medicine cure my asthma?

No. There is no cure for asthma. Although asthma cannot be cured, it can be controlled. Many medicines help people with asthma. Some are preventive medicines, and others are known as quick relievers. The preventive medicines are used for long-term control of the disease and make asthma attacks less frequent and less severe. Quick reliever medicines offer short-term relief of symptoms when asthma episodes occur.

Unless your asthma is very mild, chances are you have prescriptions for at least two different medicines. That can be confusing. The more you understand what those medicines do and why they help, the more likely you will use them correctly.

Although there are some potential unfavorable side effects from taking asthma medications, the benefit of successfully controlling your asthma outweighs the risks. It is important to discuss each of your asthma medications with your physician to learn more about their effects.

As just discussed, there are two kinds of asthma medications: long-term controllers and quick relievers.

Long-Term Control Medicines: Standard asthma treatment begins with long-term relief from anti-inflammatory drugs. These drugs make the airways less sensitive and keep them from reacting as easily to triggers. They reduce coughing, wheezing, and the struggle for breath, and they allow you to live an active life. To have long-term control of your asthma depends on you. Anti-inflammatory drugs must be taken exactly as they are prescribed.

- Cromolyn Sodium (Inhaled: Intal) and Nedocromil Sodium (Inhaled: Tilade) prevent airways from swelling when they come in contact with asthma triggers. These non-steroids can also be used to prevent asthma caused by exercise.

- Inhaled Corticosteroids ,Asmanex, Qvar Redihaler, Flovent, Pulmicort Arnuity Ellipta and Alvesco prevent and reduce airway swelling and decrease the amount of mucus in the lungs. These are generally safe when taken as directed. They are not the same as anabolic steroids, which some athletes take to build muscles. If you are taking an inhaled anti-inflammatory medicine and you feel your asthma symptoms getting worse, talk with your doctor about continuing or increasing the medicine that you are already taking. You may also need to add an oral corticosteroid or a short-acting beta antagonist (bronchodilator) for relief.

- Oral Corticosteroids (Pills or tablets: Aristocort, Celestone, Decadron, Medrol, Prednisone, Sterapred) (Liquid for children: Pediapred, Prelone) are used as a short-term treatment for severe asthma episodes or as long-term therapy for some people with severe asthma. Again, these are not the same as anabolic steroids.

- Long-acting beta-agonists (Inhaled: Serevent) is usually taken with an anti-inflammatory medicine to help control daily symptoms, including nighttime asthma. This type of medicine can also prevent asthma triggered by exercise. Because long-acting beta-agonists can not relieve symptoms quickly, they should not be used for an acute attack. It would help if you also had a short-acting, inhaled beta agonist for acute symptoms. Long-acting, inhaled beta-agonists are not a substitute for anti-inflammatory medicine. You should not decrease or stop taking your anti-inflammatory medicine without talking to your doctor, even if you feel better.

- Leukotriene modifiers (Tablets: Accolate, Singulair) are type of longterm control medication. They prevent airway inflammation and swelling, decrease mucus in the lungs, and open the airways.

- Combined therapy medicine (inhaled) contains both a controller and reliever medicine. This combination of a long-acting bronchodilator and corticosteroid is used for long-term control. Trelegy Ellipta is a triple controller inhaler, recently approved by the FDA for asthma control. It contains and inhaled steroid, long-acting bronhchodilator and long-acting anticholinergic drug.

- Anti-IgE therapy (injected) is a treatment for people with moderate or severe allergic asthma. It attempts to stop allergic asthma at its root cause instead of just treating asthma symptoms. This drug is not inhaled but rather injected by your doctor regularly. It does not eliminate your need for other asthma medications, but it can help to reduce your use of them. Due to its high cost, this form of therapy is currently reserved for moderate to severe cases requiring multiple medications.

Quick Relief Medicines

These medicines ease the wheezing, coughing and tightness of the chest that occurs during asthma episodes.

- Short-acting bronchodilators are one type of quick-relief medicine. They open airways by relaxing muscles that tighten in and around the airways during asthma episodes.

- Short-acting beta-agonists (Inhaled: Albuterol, Alupent, Brethaire, Bronkosol, Isoetharine, Maxair, Medihaler-Iso, Metaprel, Proventil, Tornalate, Ventolin, Xopenex) relieve asthma symptoms quickly, and some prevent asthma caused by exercise. If you use one of these medicines every day, or if you use it more than three times in a single day, your asthma may be getting worse, or you may not be using your inhaler correctly. Talk with your doctor right away about adding or changing medication and about your inhaler technique.

- Oral beta-agonists (Syrup, tablets, and long-acting tablets: Alupent, Brethine, Bricanyl, Proventil, Proventil Repetabs, Ventolin, Volmax) may be used for children, while long-acting tablets may be used for nighttime asthma. Oral preparations may cause more side effects than the inhaled form.

- Theophylline (Oral, slow-acting: Aerolite, Elixophyllin, Quiberon-T, Resid, Slo-bid, T-Phyl, Theolair, Theo-24, Theo-Dur, Theo-X, Uni- Dur, Uniphyl) can be used for persistently symptomatic asthma, and especially to prevent nighttime asthma. Theophylline must remain at a constant level in the bloodstream to be effective. Too high a level can be dangerous. Your doctor will order regular blood tests. Sustained release theophylline is not the preferred primary long-term control treatment, but it may be effective when added to other anti-inflammatories medicines to control nighttime episodes.

Can medicine alone help my asthma?

Unlikely. Although medicines help a lot, you cannot expect them to do the job alone. You have to help. You have to avoid the things that cause (trigger) your asthma symptoms as much as you can, even if they are things you like. In planning to avoid these triggers, you need to think about outdoor exposure as well as the triggers at home and at work that cause your problem.

Will I always have to take the same amount of medicine?

Not necessarily. You will probably take most when you begin treatment, while your doctor learns what causes your asthma, which medicine(s) control it most effectively and at what doses. Once this is completed, your medications may be reduced in number, frequency, or dose. The goal of this "step-down" method is to gain control of your asthma as quickly as possible, then maintain effective control with as little medication as necessary. Once long-term, anti-inflammatory therapy has begun, proper monitoring requires examination by a doctor every one to six months.

Will I have to take medicine all the time?

Not necessarily. Because asthma is a chronic condition that is controllable. But currently can not be cured, you will have asthma all the time, even if you are symptom-free much of the time. Your medical treatment will take into consideration the severity and frequency of your symptoms. If you have little inflammation between episodes, and if the episodes are infrequent, your treatment will emphasize quick relief from acute symptoms, particularly if they are mild.

If your symptoms occur at certain times and from a known and predictable cause, you will be treated accordingly. If, for example, you have "seasonal asthma." because of an allergy to specific pollen, you may take medicines only when pollen is in the air. But asthma so specific is uncommon, and most people with asthma take some form of medication most or all of the time.

Will medicine help me sleep better?

Yes. It is common for asthma symptoms to occur at night, and many people tell of the panic of awakening in a struggle for breath. These nighttime symptoms can be controlled with asthma medicines taken regularly. In addition, some bedding materials may be among your allergens and must be replaced with non-allergenic materials. Air filters in your bedroom may also help to maximize the benefits of your medicines if you have nighttime symptoms of asthma.

Will medicines help me breathe better when I exercise?

Yes. Physical activity, especially when combined with an irritant like cold air, may cause your airways to open and close irregularly. This is called exertion-induced bronchospasm (EIB). The short-term-relief asthma medicines, taken before and during exercise, usually control this. Thanks to these medicines, many Olympic and professional athletes enjoy successful sports careers despite their asthma.

Alternative therapies for people who have asthma and allergies

Acupuncture: A technique that involves inserting needles into key points of the body. Evidence suggests that acupuncture may signal the brain to release endorphins. These are hormones made by the body. When released, endorphins can help reduce pain and create a sense of well-being. People with asthma or allergy may experience more relaxed or calmer breathing. Users should be aware of the risk of contaminated needles or punctured organs.

Biofeedback: A technique that helps people control involuntary physical responses. Results are mixed, with children and teenagers showing the greatest benefit.

Chiropractic Spinal Manipulation: A technique that emphasizes manipulation of the spine to help the body heal itself. There is no evidence that this treatment impacts the underlying disease or pulmonary function.

Hypnosis: An artificially induced dream state that leaves the person open to suggestions, hypnosis is a legitimate technique to help people manage various conditions. Hypnosis might give people with asthma or allergies more self-discipline to follow good health practices.

Laser Treatment: A technique that uses high-intensity light to shrink swollen tissue or unblock sinuses. Laser therapy may provide temporary relief, but it may also cause scarring or other long-term physical problems.

Massage, Relaxation Techniques, Art/Music Therapy, Yoga: Stress and anxiety may cause your airways to constrict more if you have asthma or allergies. Various techniques can help you relax, reduce anxiety or control your breathing. The results may provide some benefit in helping you cope with asthma or allergy symptoms. However, evidence is not conclusive that these techniques improve lung function allergies and asthma:

ALLERGY OVERVIEW

Allergies are diseases of the immune system that cause an overreaction to substances called "allergens." Allergies are grouped by the kind of trigger, time of year, or where symptoms appear on the body: indoor and outdoor allergies (also called "hay fever," "seasonal," "perennial" or "nasal" allergies), food and drug allergies, latex allergies, insect allergies, skin allergies, and eye allergies. People who have allergies can live healthy and active lives.

What are allergies?

Allergies reflect an overreaction of the immune system to substances that usually cause no reaction in most individuals. These substances can trigger sneezing, wheezing, coughing, and itching. Allergies are not only bothersome, but many have been linked to a variety of common and serious chronic respiratory illnesses (such as sinusitis and asthma). Additionally, allergic reactions can be severe and even fatal. However, with proper management and patient education, allergic diseases can be controlled, and people with allergies can lead normal and productive lives.

Common Allergic Diseases

Allergic Rhinitis (hay fever or "indoor/outdoor," "seasonal," "perennial," or "nasal." allergies): Characterized by nasal stuffiness, sneezing, nasal itching, clear nasal discharge, and itching of the roof of the mouth and/or ears.

Allergic Asthma (asthma symptoms triggered by an allergic reaction): Characterized by airway obstruction that is at least partially reversible with medication and is always associated with allergy. Symptoms include coughing, wheezing, shortness of breath or rapid breathing, chest tightness, and occasional fatigue and slight chest pain.

Food Allergy: Most prevalent in very young children and often outgrown, a broad range of allergic reactions characterizes food allergies. Symptoms may include itching or swelling of lips or tongue; tightness of the throat with hoarseness; nausea and vomiting; diarrhea; occasional chest tightness and wheezing; itching of the eyes; decreased blood pressure or loss of consciousness and anaphylaxis.

Drug Allergy: Drug allergy is characterized by a variety of allergic responses affecting any tissue or organ. Drug allergies can cause anaphylaxis; even those patients who do not have life-threatening symptoms initially may progress to a life-threatening reaction.

Anaphylaxis (extreme response to a food, drug or insect allergy): Characterized by life-threatening symptoms. This is a medical emergency and the most severe form of allergic reaction. Symptoms include a sense of impending doom; generalized warmth or flush; tingling of palms, soles of feet or lips; light-headedness; bloating and chest tightness. These can progress into seizures, cardiac arrhythmia, shock, and respiratory distress. Possible causes can be medications, vaccines, food, latex, and insect stings and bites.

Latex Allergy: An allergic response to the proteins in natural latex rubber characterized by a range of allergic reactions. Persons at risk include healthcare workers, patients having multiple surgeries, and rubber-industry workers. Symptoms include hand dermatitis, eczema, and urticaria; sneezing, and other respiratory distress; and lower respiratory problems including coughing, wheezing, and shortness of breath.

Insect Sting/Bite Allergy: Characterized by a variety of allergic reactions; stings cannot always be avoided and can happen to anyone. Symptoms include pain, itching, and swelling at the sting site or over a larger area and can cause anaphylaxis. Insects that sting include bees, hornets, wasps, yellow jackets, and fire and harvest ants. Urticaria (hives, skin allergy): A reaction of the skin, or a skin condition commonly known as hives. Characterized by the development of itchy, raised white bumps on the skin surrounded by an area of red inflammation. Acute urticaria is often caused by an allergy to foods or medication.

Atopic Dermatitis (eczema, skin allergy): A chronic or recurrent inflammatory skin disease characterized by lesions, scaling, and flaking; it is sometimes called eczema. In children, it may be aggravated by an allergy or irritant.

Contact Dermatitis (skin allergy): Characterized by skin inflammation; this is the most common occupational disease representing up to forty percent of all occupational illnesses. Contact dermatitis is one of the most common skin diseases in adults. It results from direct contact with an outside substance with the skin. There are currently about three thousand known contact allergens.

Allergic Conjunctivitis (eye allergy): Characterized by inflammation of the eyes; it is the most common form of allergic eye disease. Symptoms can include itchy and watery eyes and lid distress. Allergic conjunctivitis is also commonly associated with other allergic diseases such as atopic dermatitis, allergic rhinitis, and asthma.

What causes allergies?

The substances that cause allergic diseases in people are known as allergens. "Antigens," or protein particles like pollen, food, or dander, enter our bodies in a variety of ways. If the antigen causes an allergic reaction, that particle is considered an "allergen"—an antigen that triggers an allergic reaction. These allergens can get into our body in several ways, including the following:

- Inhaled into the nose and the lungs. Examples are airborne pollens of certain trees, grasses, and weeds; house dust includes dust mite particles, mold spores, cat and dog dander, and latex dust.

- Ingested by mouth. Frequent culprits include shrimp, peanuts, and other nuts.

- Injected. Such as medications delivered by needle-like penicillin or other injectable drugs and venom from insect stings and bites.

- Absorbed through the skin. Plants such as poison ivy, sumac and oak, and latex are examples.

What makes some pollen cause allergies and not others?

Plant pollens carried by the wind cause most allergies to the nose, eyes, and lungs. These plants, including certain weeds, trees, and grasses, are natural pollutants produced at various times of the year when their small, inconspicuous flowers discharge billions of pollen particles.

Because the particles can be carried significant distances, it is important for you to understand not only local environmental conditions but also conditions over the broader area of the state or region in which you live. Unlike the wind-pollinated plants, conspicuous wildflowers, or flowers used in most residential gardens are pollinated by bees, wasps, and other insects and therefore are not widely capable of producing allergic diseases.

What is the role of heredity in allergy?

Like baldness, height, and eye color, the capacity to become allergic is an inherited characteristic. Yet, although you may be born with the genetic capability to become allergic, you are not automatically allergic to specific allergens.

Several of the following factors must be present for allergic sensitivity to be developed:

- The specific genes acquired from parents
- The exposure to one or more allergens to which you have a genetically programmed response
- The degree and length of exposure

A baby born with the tendency to become allergic to cow's milk, for example, may show allergic symptoms several months after birth. A genetic capability to become allergic to cat dander may take three to four years of cat exposure before the person shows symptoms. These people may also become allergic to other environmental substances with age.

On the other hand, poison ivy allergy (contact dermatitis) is an example of an allergy in which genetic background does not play a part. The person with poison ivy allergy first has to be exposed to the oil from the plant. This usually occurs during youth, when a rash does not always appear. However, the first exposure may sensitize or cause the person to become allergic and, when subsequent exposure takes place, a contact dermatitis rash appears and can be quite severe. Many plants are capable of producing this type of rash. Substances other than plants, such as dyes, metals, and chemicals in deodorants and cosmetics, can also cause similar dermatitis.

Diagnosis

If you break out in hives when a bee stings you, or you sneeze every time you pet a cat, you know what some of your allergens are. But if the pattern is not so obvious, try keeping a record of when, where, and under what circumstances your reactions occur. This can be as easy as jotting down notes on a calendar. If the pattern still isn't clear, make an appointment with your doctor for help.

Doctors diagnose allergies in three steps:

1. Personal and medical history. Your doctor will ask you questions to get a complete understanding of your symptoms and their possible causes. Bring your notes to help jog your memory. Be ready to answer questions about your family history, the kinds of medicines you take, and your lifestyle at home, school, and work

2. Physical examination. If your doctor suspects an allergy, he or she will pay special attention to your ears, eyes, nose, throat, chest, and skin during the physical examination. This exam may include a pulmonary function test to detect how well you exhale air from your lungs. You may also need an x-ray of your lungs or sinuses.

3. Tests to determine your allergens. Your doctor may do a skin test, patch test, or blood test.

Scratch Skin Test: For most people, skin tests are the most accurate and least expensive way to confirm suspected allergens. There are two types of allergen skin tests. In prick/scratch testing, a small drop of the possible allergen is placed on the skin, followed by lightly pricking or scratching with a needle through the drop. An intradermal (under the skin) testing, a very small amount of allergen is injected into the outer layer of skin.

With either test, if you are allergic to the substance, you will develop redness, swelling, and itching at the test site within twenty minutes. You may also see a "wheel" or raised, round area that looks like a hive. Usually, the larger the wheel, the more sensitive you are to the allergen.

Patch Test: This test determines if you have contact dermatitis. Your doctor will place a small amount of a possible allergen on your skin, cover it with a bandage, and check your reaction after forty-eight to seventy-two hours. If you are allergic to the substance, you should develop a rash.

Blood Tests: Allergen blood tests (also called radioallergosorbent tests [RAST], enzyme-linked immunosorbent assays [ELISA], fluorescent allergosorbent tests [FAST], multiple radioallergosorbent tests [MAST], or radioimmunosorbent tests [RIST]) are sometimes used when people have a skin condition or are taking medicines that interfere with skin testing. Your doctor will take a blood sample and send it to a laboratory. The lab adds the allergen to your blood sample, and then measures the number of specific IgE antibodies your blood produces to attack the allergens.

Treatment

Good allergy treatment is based on the results of your allergy tests, your medical history, and the severity of your symptoms. It can include three different treatment strategies: avoidance of allergens, medication options, and/ or immunotherapy (allergy shots).

Medication

Some people don't take allergy medicines because they don't take their symptoms seriously ("Oh, it's only my allergies."). The result may be painful complications such as sinus or ear infections. Don't take the risk. There are so many safe prescription and non-prescription medicines to relieve allergy symptoms. The following is a brief list of medications taken for allergies. They are available in non-prescription and prescription forms.

- Antihistamines and decongestants are the most common medicines used for allergies. Antihistamines help relieve rashes and hives, as well as sneezing, itching, and runny nose. Prescription antihistamines are similar to their non-prescription counterparts, but many of them do not cause drowsiness. Decongestant pills, sprays, and nose drops reduce stuffiness by shrinking swollen membranes in the nose.

- It is important to remember that using a non-prescription nasal decongestant spray more than three days in a row may cause swelling and stuffiness in your nose to become worse, even after you stop using the medicine. This is called a "rebound" reaction. Some non-prescription "cold" medicines combine an antihistamine, a pain reliever like aspirin or acetaminophen, and a decongestant. Aspirin can cause asthma attacks in some people. Don't take a chance:

- If you have asthma, talk with your doctor before taking any non-prescription allergy medicine.

- Eye drops may provide temporary relief from burning or bloodshot eyes. There are several over-the-counter eyedrops that contain antihistamines and can safely be used. The problem is that some contain topical decongestants (to clear the eyes or reddening) and if overused may increase ocular pressure. These are usually vasoconstrictors vs antihistamines.

- Corticosteroid creams or ointments relieve itchiness and halt the spread of rashes. Corticosteroids are not the same as anabolic steroids that are used illegally by some athletes to build muscles. If your rash does not go away after using a non-prescription corticosteroid for (a week?), see your doctor.

- Corticosteroid nasal sprays help reduce the inflammation that causes nasal congestion without the chance of the "rebound" effect found in non-prescription nose sprays.

- Cromolyn sodium prevents inflammation which causes nasal congestion. Because it has few, if any, side effects, cromolyn can be safely used over long periods.

- Oral corticosteroids may be prescribed to reduce swelling and stop severe allergic reactions. Because these medications can cause serious side effects, you should expect your doctor to monitor you carefully.

- Epinephrine comes in pre-measured, self-injectable containers and is the most important medication that can help during a life-threatening anaphylactic attack. To be effective, epinephrine must be given within minutes of the first sign of a serious allergic reaction.

Note: New prescription and non-prescription drugs are approved periodically. If the prescription you are taking is not on this list, ask your doctor which category (above) it falls into so that you can refer to this information.

Living With Allergic Asthma

Make life with allergic asthma a little easier by avoiding the things you're allergic to. Sound like common sense? Sure it does. Unfortunately, trying to put this advice into practice in your everyday life is not always practical. For example, to completely avoid ragweed pollen, you couldn't go outdoors from August to November. There are, however, a few steps you can take that are more realistic and can be very helpful. To help lessen the allergic reactions that cause your asthma symptoms, familiarize yourself with the following strategies for avoiding allergens from cockroaches, dust mites, mold spores, and pet dander.

Cockroaches

- Limit where you eat to avoid spreading food and crumbs around the house and always keep food out of bedrooms.

- Keep all food and garbage in closed containers. Never leave food out.

- Wash the kitchen floor and countertops at least once a week.

- Repair leaky faucets and drainpipes to eliminate water sources that attract these pests.

- Close up all openings around the house that might allow cockroaches to enter.

- Reduce the number of cockroaches by using environmentally safe pesticides and bait stations.

Dust Mites

- Encase your mattress and pillows in dust-proof or allergen impermeable covers (available from mail-order specialty supply companies, as well as some bedding and department stores).

- Wash all bedding and blankets once a week in hot water (at least 130– 140° F) to kill dust mites. Replace wool or feathered bedding with synthetic materials, and make sure all stuffed animals are washable.

- Replace wall-to-wall carpets in bedrooms with bare floors (linoleum, tile, or wood) if possible.

- Use a damp mop or rag to remove dust from surfaces. Never use a dry cloth, which just stirs up mite allergens..

- Use a dehumidifier or air conditioner to maintain relative humidity at fifty percent or below.

- Use a vacuum cleaner with either a double-layered microfilter bag or a high-efficiency particulate air (HEPA) filter to trap allergens that pass through a vacuum's exhaust.

Mold Spores

- Use a dehumidifier or air conditioner to maintain relative humidity below fifty percent and keep temperatures cool.

- Vent clothes dryers and bathrooms to the outside so that moisture does not accumulate in your home.

- Check faucets, pipes, and ductwork for leaks.

- Leave the room or drive with the windows open for several minutes to allow mold spores to disperse after you turn on air conditioners in your home or car.

- Remove decaying debris from the yard, roof, and gutters.

- Avoid raking leaves, mowing lawns, and working with peat, mulch, hay, or dead wood. If you must do yard work, wear a mask and avoid working on hot, humid days.

Pet Dander

- Remove all pets from your home if possible.

- Keep pets confined to areas without carpets or upholstered furniture and out of bedrooms if it is not possible to remove the animals.

- Wear a dust mask and gloves when near any rodents such as mice, hamsters, guinea pigs, squirrels, etc.

- Wash your hands and clean your clothes after playing with your pet— this will remove pet allergens.

- Ask someone else to clean soiled litter cages when possible.

- Dust regularly with a damp cloth.

ASTHMA AND ECZEMA

Asthma and eczema are both linked to inflammation. Research suggests you may be more likely than most people to have the other if you have one condition. Not everyone with asthma has eczema. But there's a strong link between having eczema as a child and developing asthma later on in life.

There's no single explanation for this association. Early allergen exposure and genes may contribute.

Here's what researchers currently know about the link between asthma and eczema, along with tips to manage both conditions.

The link between eczema and asthma

Both eczema and asthma are linked to inflammation that's often caused by a strong reaction to environmental allergens.

Half of all people with moderate to severe eczema also have:

- Asthma
- Allergic rhinitis
- Food allergies

One study found that babies diagnosed with eczema in the first two years of life were three times more likely to develop asthma and rhinitis within the next five years than those who didn't have infant eczema. Other research has reached similar conclusions.

Eczema, or atopic dermatitis, is an inflammatory skin condition where your immune system tends to overreact to an environmental trigger. The condition tends to run in families. Inheriting a filaggrin gene mutation from your parents can lead to a "leaky" skin barrier that reduces your skin's ability to block allergens and allows moisture to escape.

This causes eczema symptoms like dry and irritated skin. Allergens, such as pollen, dander, and dust mites, contain enzymes that may also break down the skin's barrier. The wheezing, coughing, and chest tightness associated with asthma are often caused by a strong immune response to environmental allergens.

Inflammation causes the airways to swell and narrow, leading to breathing problems. The exact causes of asthma are unknown and vary from person to person. Genes may play a role in the immune system's strong reaction.

What role do allergies play in eczema and asthma asthma attacks?

Allergic reactions occur when your immune system overreacts to certain benign substances it sees as harmful. One unintended consequence of this response is increased inflammation in your body. Your immune system releases antibodies as well as chemicals called histamines to combat these triggers. Histamine is responsible for classic allergy symptoms such as:

- Sneezing
- Runny nose
- Nasal congestion
- Itchy skin
- Hives and skin rashes
- Itchy, watery eyes

Allergies may cause several types of immune reactions in some people. It's common for inhalant allergens to trigger both allergic asthma and eczema.

Studies have increasingly linked eczema from inhalant allergens to a decrease in lung function. Examples of inhalant allergens include:

- Dust mites
- Pollen
- Mold
- Animal dander

Many other triggers besides allergens can cause asthma and eczema flare-ups. You'll notice that some triggers can aggravate both asthma and eczema.

Possible eczema triggers include:
- Cold or dry air
- Stress
- Bacterial or viral skin infections
- Irritants found in detergents, soaps, fragrances, chemicals, and smoke, heat ,and humidity

The following may trigger asthma flare-ups:
- Cold or dry air
- Stress
- Upper respiratory infections
- Irritants like smoke, air pollution, or strong odors heartburn
- Exercise

Managing eczema and asthma

If you have both eczema and asthma, it's important to ask your allergist about allergy testing. A history of eczema could mean you're more likely to develop allergic rhinitis and allergic asthma.

Even if you had allergy tests as a child, you could develop new allergies as an adult. Knowing your triggers can help minimize symptoms of eczema and asthma. Once you know your triggers, it's important to reduce your daily contact with allergens as much as possible. You can start by:

- Using an air conditioner in your home
- Keeping windows closed
- Washing your bedding weekly in hot water
- Vacuuming carpets and rugs once a week
- Keeping pets out of your bedroom
- Taking showers immediately after you've been outdoors and before bedtime
- Maintaining a humidity below forty to fifty percent in your home

If lifestyle changes and medications aren't enough to manage your allergy-induced asthma and eczema, some treatments may help address both conditions. These include:

Immunotherapy. Regular allergy shots may help treat allergic asthma and eczema by introducing your immune system to tiny amounts of allergens. Your immune system builds up a tolerance until you experience fewer symptoms after three to five years of treatments.

Biologic medications. This daily pill helps reduce allergy and asthma symptoms by controlling the chemicals your immune system releases when you encounter an allergen. It's unclear if it helps treat eczema.

Leukotriene modifiers (montelukast). This daily pill helps reduce allergy and asthma symptoms by controlling the chemicals your immune system releases when you encounter an allergen. It's unclear if it helps treat eczema.

Talk to your allergist about which treatments might be right for you.

OSTEOPOROSIS

What Is Osteoporosis?

Osteoporosis is a serious condition in which bones become thin, brittle, and easily broken. The National Osteoporosis Foundation (NOF) estimates that more than forty-four million Americans have osteoporosis or low bone density placing them at risk for osteoporosis. This represents fifty-five percent of people aged fifty and older in the United States. While most affected by osteoporosis are women, one in eight men also suffers from the disease. This rate is expected to increase as men live longer. Similarly, while osteoporosis is more prevalent in Caucasian and Asian populations, African Americans and Latinos are also at significant risk of developing the disease. Osteoporosis is called the "silent disease" because people do not know that they have osteoporosis until their bones become so weak that a sudden strain, bump, a fall, or even a sneeze can cause a fracture.

The most common fractures associated with osteoporosis include the wrist, vertebral and hip fractures. It is estimated that half of all women and twenty percent of all men will have an osteoporotic fracture in their lifetime. In the United States, three thousand hip fractures occur each year in persons age sixty-five and older. The majority of these hip fractures are associated with a fall in an individual with osteoporosis.

Osteoporosis is a pediatric disease with geriatric consequences. Peak bone mass is built during our first three decades. Failure to build strong bones during childhood and adolescent years manifests in fractures later in life. The good news is that osteoporosis is both preventable and treatable. Steps can be taken at any age to prevent or minimize the effect of osteoporosis.

Asthma and Osteoporosis

The Asthma-Osteoporosis Connection: Millions of men, women, and children who have arthritis, asthma, or other diseases take corticosteroids, often resulting in the development of osteoporosis. Powerful anti-inflammatory drugs such as prednisone and cortisone greatly increase the risk of developing osteoporosis. This bone-thinning disease leads to painful fractures, loss of height and independence, and can even lead to death. Check with your health care provider or pharmacist if you are taking asthma, arthritis, anti-inflammatory, or anti-convulsant drugs.

Asthma And Bone Loss: Asthma affects between twenty-five million Americans, more than four million of whom are under the age of eighteen. Asthma is becoming more common, with African Americans, especially at risk. People with asthma are at increased risk for osteoporosis, especially in the spine. Anti-inflammatory medications are taken by mouth decrease calcium absorbed from food, increase calcium loss from the kidneys, and decrease bone formation. Corticosteroids also interfere with the production of sex hormones in both women and men, contributing to bone loss and causing muscle weakness, both of which can increase the risk of falling.

Asthma medication can increase the risk of osteoporosis. People with asthma treated with forty to sixty mg per day of oral corticosteroids for long periods are most likely to experience bone loss. Even those patients taking ten mg per day are likely to experience some bone loss over time. Bone loss increases with increased glucocorticoid doses and prolonged use.

Asthmatics who use corticosteroids to manage their asthma are at significant risk for bone loss and should ask their doctor about a bone density test to measure their current bone mass and diagnose osteoporosis before fractures occur.

Asthma And Osteoporosis Medications: Maintaining appropriate hormone levels of estrogen in women and testosterone in men will help maintain optimal bone health. At menopause, estrogen replacement therapy (ERT) or hormone replacement therapy (HRT) may effectively prevent bone loss and osteoporosis resulting from corticosteroid use. Other medications to stop bone loss include Fosamax (alendronate), Miacalcin (calcitonin), Actonel (risedronate), and Evista (raloxifene).

Calcium And Asthma: Many people living with asthma think that milk and dairy products trigger asthmatic attacks. I suggest you talk to your doctors about non-dietary sources of calcium like leafy green vegetables, soy products and fortified non-dairy beverages and other food.

Exercise And Asthma: Physical exercise can trigger an asthma attack, and many people with asthma avoid weight-bearing physical activities that can strengthen the bone. Weight-bearing exercises that work the body against gravity, such as walking, racquet sports, basketball, volleyball, aerobics, dancing, or weight training, can improve bone health. Talk to your health care provider or ask for a referral to the physical therapist. Consult a physical therapist about the best types of exercise before beginning an exercise program.

Calcium And Vitamin D

To build strong bones, make sure you get enough calcium at every age. Make sure you're taking enough calcium in your daily diet. The first choice for adequate calcium intake is from food.

- Make it a habit, to take your calcium at the same times each day, such as when you finish meals or brush your teeth.

- Remember to eat foods with calcium several times throughout the day; your body uses calcium best when it can absorb it in small doses.

- Build strong bones by taking Vitamin D. You need 400-800 International Units each day.

- Take calcium because it plays an important role in keeping bones strong, but calcium alone cannot prevent or cure osteoporosis.

- Maintain proper nutrition and adequate calcium can help if you have osteoporosis. Exercise can help, too.

Calcium To Prevent Bone

Loss: Calcium and vitamin D in your diet protects the calcium in your bones. If you are not getting enough calcium, your bones become your body's emergency supply of calcium. When this happens, your bones become weak and break easily.

Many women consume less then half of the daily recommended amount of calcium. Calcium alone cannot prevent or cure osteoporosis, but it is an important part of preventing osteoporosis.

Foods Rich In Calcium And Vitamin D: Vitamin D plays a major role in calcium absorption and bone health. Vitamin D allows calcium to leave the intestine and enter the bloodstream. Vitamin D can be found in leafy green vegetables and soybean based products, D-fortified dairy products, egg yolks, saltwater fish, and liver. Vitamin D is manufactured in the skin following direct exposure to sunlight. About ten to fifteen minutes of sunlight on your hands, arms, and face two or three times a week may meet the body's needs for vitamin D. It depends on the time of year, location, amount of melanin in the skin, whether using sunblock etc. Since sunscreen diminishes the body's ability to manufacture Vitamin D, spend your first ten to fifteen minutes without sunscreen, then be sure to put on sunscreen for the remainder of your time outdoors. Remember, sunlight helps build strong bones

Vitamin D: Vitamin D plays a major role in calcium absorption and bone health. Vitamin D3 is manufactured in the skin following direct exposure to sunlight; however, many different factors affect a person's ability to make adequate amounts of Vitamin D. Vitamin D is critical for health, especially for bone health. Vitamin D is a term used to name several forms of related compounds. All are fat-soluble and act to control calcium metabolism. Vitamin D is vital to the absorption of calcium. But how Vitamin D works is complicated. The various parts of Vitamin D metabolism happen throughout the body.

As little as ten minutes of sunshine can make Vitamin D3 in the skin. But in New Jersey, the sun's angle is only in the right place from about the end of April through the middle of October. Which means one needs to sit in the sun with their skin exposed and without sunscreen. In the winter in the northeast, when the sun is too low, a dietary intake of Vitamin D becomes the sole source during those months. Vitamin D3, either consumed in the diet or made in the skin, is stored in the liver.

Food Sources: Vitamin D can be obtained from fortified milk, egg yolks, saltwater fish, and liver. Some foods may be fortified with Vitamin D, including cereals, breakfast bars, milk alternatives, or supplements.

Supplements: Usually, Vitamin D is supplied in tablets in the D3 form, known as cholecalciferol.

Osteoporosis exercise guideline

- Calcium citrate (e.g., Citracal) is often added to breakfast products and juice. It's easier to absorb, but it contains the lowest amount of calcium, and it is usually the most costly.

- Calcium phosphate (e.g., Posture) is easily absorbed and does not have to be taken with food, but has excessive phosphorus.

- Calcium lactate—avoid this form if dairy intolerant• Calcium gluconate requires many pills to get recommended minimum dose of calcium.

- Dolomite, bone meal may be contaminated with lead, so should be avoided.

Vitamin D: Vitamin D plays a major role in calcium absorption and bone health. Vitamin D3 is manufactured in the skin following direct exposure to sunlight; however, many different factors affect a person's ability to make adequate amounts of Vitamin D. Vitamin D is critical for health, especially for bone health. Vitamin D is a term used to name several forms of related compounds. All are fat-soluble and act to control calcium metabolism. Vitamin D is vital to the absorption of calcium. But how Vitamin D works are complicated. The various parts of Vitamin D metabolism happen throughout the body.

As little as ten minutes of sunshine can make Vitamin D3 in the skin. But in New Jersey, the sun's angle is only in the right place from about the end of April through the middle of October. You need to sit in the sun with your skin exposed without sunscreen, of course. In the winter in the northeast, when the sun is too low, a dietary intake of Vitamin D becomes the sole source during those months. Vitamin D3, either consumed in the diet or made in the skin, is stored in the liver.

Food Sources: Vitamin D can be obtained from fortified milk, egg yolks, saltwater fish, and liver. Some foods may be fortified with Vitamin D, including cereals, breakfast bars, milk alternatives, or supplements.

Supplements: Usually, Vitamin D is supplied in tablets in the D3 form, known as cholecalciferol.

Osteoporosis exercise guideline

- Check with your physician concerning any restrictions you may have before beginning an exercise program.

- Avoid any exercise that causes or increases pain.

- Stop exercising if you feel dizzy or short of breath.

- Do nothold your breath while exercising.

- Make sure to keep your body in alignment when performing all exercises.

- Avoid exercises that involve forward bending of your spine (i.e., toe touches, sit-ups). These exercises can increase the incidence of vertebral fractures.

- Avoid exercises that involve excessive twisting (i.e., windmill toe touches). This puts too much force on your spine.

- Do resistance exercises. Free weights, exercise machines, and resistance bands are examples of this type of exercise. Strive to do one set of eight to ten repetitions of each resistance exercise. For a more challenging program, progress to three sets of eight to ten repetitions.

- Rest one to two minutes between sets of exercises when using weights.

- Start with one-pound weights, then gradually increase the amount of weight when using weights. Too much weight can be harmful.

- Wear shoes with good support and cushioning while exercising. Replace shoes when cushioning begins to wear out.

Increase Your Exercise: Physical activity throughout life helps develop and maintain strong bones and decreases bone loss. Persons age thirty-five and older should consult their physician before beginning an exercise program. Your health care provider can make a referral to a physical therapist. Before you exercise, consult a physical therapist about the best types of exercise. The complete osteoporosis exercise program should include weight-bearing, resistance, postural, and balance exercises. It is important to check with your physician or physical therapist before starting any exercise program.

Weight-bearing exercises use the weight of the body to work against gravity and are recommended for all ages. Your bones respond to this force by growing stronger. Walking, jogging, dancing, hiking, stair climbing, and aerobic exercises are all examples of weight-bearing exercises. The goal is to work up to forty-five minutes or more per session. Perform these exercises at least three to five times per week. (Bike riding and swimming, although good practices are not weight-bearing activities).

Resistance exercises generate muscle tension on the bones and are recommended for everyone after the age of fourteen. Resistance exercise strengthens the muscles and stimulates the bones to grow stronger. Free weights, exercise machines, and resistance bands are examples of this type of exercise. Start exercising without weights. Begin with one set of eight to ten repetitions of each exercise, increasing gradually to three sets. When that becomes easy, add one lb. of weight at a time. These exercises should be done two to three times a week but not on consecutive days.

Postural exercises decrease harmful stress on the back. By performing these exercises, you can reduce your risk of spinal fractures and the rounded shoulders commonly seen with osteoporosis. These exercises should be performed throughout the day to reinforce good posture. Balance exercises help maintain equilibrium and reduce the risk of falling. These exercises should be performed daily.

Exercise And The Role Of The Physical Therapist:

A physical therapist can design an exercise program that is safe and appropriate for both prevention and treatment of osteoporosis. Physical therapists are trained to teach proper ways to perform daily activities to reduce fracture risk. Talk to your physician about a referral to a physical therapist. Many individuals with osteoporosis will have postural changes, muscle, and soft tissue tightness that requires the hands-on treatment of a physical therapist.

LIVING WITH ASTHMA

Asthma is a long-term disease that requires long-term care. Successful asthma treatment requires you to take an active role in your care and follow your asthma action plan.

Learn How To Manage Your Asthma

Partner with your doctor to develop an asthma action plan. This plan will help you to take your medicines, identify your asthma triggers properly, and manage your disease if asthma symptoms worsen. Children age ten or older— and younger children who can handle it—should be involved in developing and following their asthma action plan.

Most people who have asthma can successfully manage their symptoms at home by following their asthma action plans and having regular checkups. However, it's important to know when to seek emergency medical care. Learn how to use your medicines correctly. If you take inhaled medicines, you should practice using your inhaler at your doctor's office. If you take long-term control medicines, take them daily as your doctor prescribes. Record your asthma symptoms as a way to track how well your asthma is controlled. Also, you may use a peak flow meter to measure and record how well your lungs are working.

Your doctor may ask you to keep records of your symptoms or peak flow results daily for a couple of weeks before an office visit and bring these records with you to the visit

These steps will help you keep track overtime of how well you're controlling your asthma. This will help you spot problems early and prevent or relieve asthma attacks. Recording your symptoms and peak flow results to share with your doctor also will help your doctor decides whether to adjust your treatment.

Ongoing Care

Have regular asthma checkups with your doctor so he or she can assess your level of asthma control and adjust your treatment if needed. Remember, the main goal of asthma treatment is to achieve the best control of your asthma using the least amount of medicine. This may require frequent adjustments to your treatments.

If it's hard to follow your plan or the plan isn't working well, let your health care team know right away. They will work with you to adjust your plan to suit your needs better. Get treatment for any other conditions that can interfere with your asthma management.

Watch For Signs That Your Asthma Is Getting Worse

Here are some signs that your asthma may be getting worse:

- Your symptoms start to occur more often, are more severe, and/or bother you at night and cause you to lose sleep.

- You're limiting your normal activities and missing school or work because of your asthma.

- Your peak flow number is low compared to your personal best or varies a lot from day today.

- Your asthma medicines don't seem to work well anymore.

- You have to use your quick-relief inhaler more often. If you're using quick-relief medicine more than two days a week, your asthma isn't well controlled.

- You have to go to the emergency room or doctor because of an asthma attack.

If you have any of these signs, see your doctor. He or she may need to change your medicines or take other steps to control your asthma. Partner with your health care team and take an active role in your care. This can help control asthma, so it doesn't interfere with your activities and disrupt your life.

RECOGNIZING ASTHMA SYMPTOMS AND TRIGGERS

What are the signs and symptoms of asthma?

Common asthma symptoms include the following:

- Coughing: Coughing from asthma is often worse at night or early in the morning, making it hard to sleep.

- Wheezing: Wheezing is a whistling or squeaky sound that occurs when you breathe.

- Chest Tightness: This may feel like something is squeezing or sitting on your chest.

- Shortness of Breath: Some people who have asthma say they can't catch their breath or feel out of breath. You may feel like you can't get the air out of your lungs.

Not all people who have asthma have these symptoms. Likewise, having these symptoms doesn't always mean that you have asthma. A lung function test, done along with a medical history (including type and frequency of your symptoms) and physical exam, is the best way to diagnose asthma. With certain types of asthma symptoms the frequency and severity, may vary over time. Sometimes your symptoms may just annoy you. Other times they may be troublesome enough to limit your daily routine. Severe symptoms can threaten your life. It's vital to treat symptoms when you first notice them, so they don't become severe. With proper treatment, most people who have asthma can expect to have few, if any, symptoms either during the day or at night.

What causes asthma symptoms to occur?

Several things can bring about or cause. your asthma symptoms to get worse. Your doctor will help you find out which things (sometimes called triggers) may cause your asthma to flare up if you come in contact with them. Triggers may include the following:

- Allergens found in dust, animal fur, cockroaches, mold, and pollens from trees, grasses, and flowers;

- Irritants such as cigarette smoke, air pollution, chemicals, or dust in the workplace, compounds in home décor products, and sprays (such as hairspray);

- Certain medicines such as aspirin or other nonsteroidal anti-inflammatories drugs and nonselective beta-blockers;

- Sulfites in foods and drinks;

- Viral upper respiratory infections such as colds; or

- Exercise (physical activity).

Other health conditions—such as runny nose, sinus infections, reflux disease, psychological stress, and sleep apnea—can make asthma more difficult to manage. These conditions need treatment as part of an overall asthma care plan.

Asthma is different for each person. Some of the factors listed may not affect you. Other factors that do affect you may not be on the list. Talk to your doctor about the things that seem to make your asthma worse

Stress And Asthma

There are Many stressors that affect asthma control in patients with asthma. These include allergens (such as cat dander and pollen), irritants (e.g., smoke), and cold infections. These are usually considered 'exposures,' and we try to identify these triggers and avoid them if we can. Similarly, stress can be thought of as a type of exposure, though a psychological one, which can trigger asthma. Many patients find that stressful situations make them feel short of breath and wheeze and that they need to use their quick relief inhaler for relief.

Stressful life events, which are less immediate, can also lead to decrease asthma control in certain individuals. A recent study measured quality of life related to asthma in a range of individuals and found that in people with similar baseline asthma severity, asthma control was poorer in subsets of individuals who had recent stressful life events, such as divorce or moving. Another study in children found that the beneficial response to sublingual immunotherapy (similar to allergy shots) was decreased in children with stressful lives and life events. While the mechanism by which stress and stressful life events decrease asthma control, clinic and research studies show that the connection is clear.

What About Stress And Asthma In Animal Models

To better understand this connection, researchers have tried to replicate what is known in humans using animal models. In an animal model of asthma in mice, studies have shown that stressing animals leads to changes in the asthmatic response. These changes were found at different stages of developing asthma in these models, both early and late. Researchers hope that these models of stress and asthma will improve our understanding of the way that stress causes decrease asthma control.

Closing Thoughts

Avoiding stress is not an easy trigger to avoid, not as easy as other asthma triggers, such as pets and pollens. But being aware of this direct connection is important for all patients with asthma. Your doctor can help you to better control your asthma, especially for triggers that are less typical and, like stress, poorly understood

AIR POLLUTION AND OUTDOOR TRIGGERS

When you're outdoors, you have less control over the triggers you encounter. You can't, for example, vacuum the lawn if pollen is bothering you, and there's no air cleaner large enough to clean a city's air pollution. Still, there are things you can do to help reduce your exposure to outdoor triggers. By making a few adjustments and by taking your medication as directed, you can breathe easier when you're outside.

Molds

Molds are asthma triggers for many people. A type of fungus, its spores float in the air where they're easily inhaled and can lead to coughing, sneezing, wheezing and chest tightness. You'll find molds wherever it's damp. This includes piles of vegetation, stagnant water, and garbage containers.

Pollens

Pollens are a very common trigger for asthma symptoms. Generated by trees, grasses, and weeds, airborne pollens are easily inhaled, especially during warm-weather months. If you're allergic to pollen, there are several things you can do to stay healthy:

- Use a HEPA-filtered air cleaner.

- Plant low-allergen gardens.
- On days when the pollen count is high, use an air conditioner in your home and car, and also try to keep your windows closed as much as possible.
- Consider exercising inside on days when the the pollen count is high if you usually exercise outdoors.
- Avoid going outside between 5 a.m. and 10 a.m. on hot and windy days.
- Check the pollen count to see whether you should reduce the amount of time you spend outdoors.
- Shower and change your clothing if you've been outdoors on high pollen- count day.
- Remove plants in your yard that trigger symptoms.
- Use a good furnace filter and change it regularly.
- Do not place trees or plants near windows or near the air-intake of your furnace or air conditioner.
- Do not hang your laundry out to dry. Use a clothes dryer instead.
- Do not touch plants that you think might be triggers and if you do, wash your hands immediately afterward.

Cold Air

Cold air, or sudden changes in the weather, can also trigger asthma symptoms. If you're affected by the cold, the following tips can help:

- Try breathing through your nose. This helps warm the air before it reaches your lungs.
- Wear a scarf or a special cold-weather mask to help humidify and warm the air you breathe, making it easier on your lungs if you have to breathe through your mouth..
- Exercise indoors on cold days.

Air Pollutants

While air pollution as a cause of asthma has not been verified, there is good evidence that pollution causes the symptoms of many people with asthma to get worse on days when the air quality index is high. If you find your symptoms become worse on these days, try to:

- Reduce the amount of time you spend outside when air pollution is high;
- Exercise indoors if you usually exercise outdoors;
- Turn on the air conditioner in your home and car and keep your windows closed.

Outdoor Air Pollution

Small particles and ozone come from the exhaust from cars and factories, smoke, and road dust. When inhaled, outdoor pollutants can aggravate the lungs and lead to chest pain, coughing, shortness of breath, and throat irritation. Outdoor air pollution may also worsen chronic respiratory diseases, such as asthma. When ozone air pollution is highest, it has been associated with ten–twenty percent of all respiratory hospital visits and admissions.

Watch for the Air Quality Index, or AQI, during your local weather report. The AQI is a tool that offers you clear information every day on whether air quality in your area could be a health risk. The AQI uses colors to show how much pollution is in the air. Green and yellow mean air pollution levels are low. Orange, red, or purple mean pollution is at levels that may make asthma worse.

Actions You Can Take: State agencies will use television and radio to notify citizens of ozone alerts. On days when your state or local air pollution control agency calls an Ozone Action Day, people with asthma should limit prolonged physical activity outdoors. Consider adjusting outdoor activities to early in the morning or later in the evening.

CONTROLLING ASTHMA TRIGGERS IN THE HOME

Indoor Triggers—Home And Work

With smog, pollen, and severe weather changes, you might think that you're more likely to encounter more triggers outdoors than indoors. In fact, the opposite is true. Canadians spend ninety percent of their time indoors. This, along with changes in how our homes are built, leads to poor indoor air quality and more triggers in our homes.

Fortunately, a great deal has been learned about asthma triggers that exist inside. By educating yourself about indoor hazards, you'll discover simple ways to reduce their levels.

Dust Mites: Dust mite allergy is a common problem for people with asthma. The excretions and body parts of these tiny, spider-like creatures can be a powerful trigger of asthma symptoms.

Dust mites congregate in soft-surfaced places where there is an abundant food supply. Dust mites feed off shed human skin and are thus found in bedding, mattresses, pillows, sofas and carpets.

Effective strategies for minimizing dust mites are:
- Use a dehumidifier in the damp area. Keep the humidity level below fifty percent. Dust mites can't survive in dry environments.
- Remove carpets, especially in the bedroom;

- Launder bed linens in very hot water (131 degrees Fahrenheit).
- Encase your pillow, mattress, and box spring in mite-allergen impermeable casings.

Cockroaches: Cockroaches are one of the most hated household pests, and for a good reason. Not only are they a terrible nuisance, but their faces have also been shown to trigger symptoms in individuals with asthma.

If your home has cockroaches, make sure that food and water are never left where they can get at them. To ensure they leave and never come back, call a professional exterminator.

Indoor Molds: molds are fungus that can be found just about anywhere it's damp and where airflow is minimal, like basements and bathrooms. Their airborne spores can trigger asthma symptoms, but there are many ways to avoid them. The best way is to keep your home dry and clean.

- Monitor the humidity level in your home with a hygrometer and keep the level between forty–forty-five percent.
- Make sure your home is well ventilated.
- Remove carpeting where possible. If carpet is kept, vacuum thoroughly and frequently using a vacuum cleaner with a high-efficiency particulate air (HEPA) filter.
- Clean moldy areas, especially in bathrooms, with an anti-mold cleaner like vinegar or a chlorine-bleach solution. When using these chemicals, be sure to use them in a well-ventilated area.
- Ensure that you have proper drainage around your house.
- Use a dehumidifier if humidity is higher than fifty percent (basements).
- Use bathroom and kitchen fans always.
- Reduce your number of house plants.

- Do not have carpet in bathrooms or directly on concrete floors in the basement.

Chemical Fumes: Many people with asthma are affected by airborne chemicals. They may be exposed to them in the home or even at work.

At home, chemicals are reasonably easy to control. If you have paints or other volatile products in your house, you can get rid of them or seal them carefully and place them in a garage or shed. If you're sensitive to heavy perfumes, try not to use products that contain them.

Occupational Asthma: If you have any of the following jobs, you may be at risk for occupational asthma

- Grains, flours, plants and gums: Bakers, chemists, and farmers
- Animals, insects and fungi: Poultry workers, entomologists, laboratory workers, and veterinary professionals
- Chemicals: Aircraft fitters, brewery workers, pulp mill workers, electronic workers, hair stylist, refrigeration workers, resin manufacturers and dye weighers
- Isocyanates and metals: Car sprayers, boat builders, foam, TDI [tluene diisocyanate] and refrigerator manufacturers, platinum chemists and refiners, printers and laminators, and welders
- Drugs and enzymes: Ampicillin, detergent and enzyme manufacturers, pharmacists and pharmaceutical workers
- Woods: Carpenters, millers, saw-mill workers, wood finishers and machinists.

THE BACK-TO-SCHOOL SEASON AND ASTHMA

In this chapter, we discuss some things to think about as families go back to school in terms of asthma. One is the increase in asthma exacerbations during this period, and the other some thoughts about asthma control as kids go back to school.

Asthma Gets Worse In September

For several years, doctors and patients have observed that asthma attacks, including asthma exacerbations, increase in September. Some doctors and scientists have even called the increase in hospitalizations for asthma the "September Epidemic."

The reason for this remained obscure until recent studies that looked into the major causes of worsening asthma control and if they changed in September. It turns out that the increase in asthma attacks and kids going back to school are not merely coincidences. A detailed study of asthma attacks looking at many individuals (using twelve years of hospitalization data from the Canadian health ministry) showed a sharp spike in asthma hospitalization in children about two weeks after Labor Day, the usual time of school return after summer vacation.

Even more interesting was the fact that asthma exacerbations were also increased in adults, not just children. Of note, this increase occurred about a week later than in children.

So, What Is The Connection?

It is well known that respiratory viral infections, especially a common cold virus called rhinovirus, are significant causes of asthma exacerbations. A parallel study to the one above demonstrated that nearly two-thirds of children seeking emergency care for asthma had the common cold virus in their noses. This suggests that the September Epidemic is largely caused by cold viruses. In addition, the delay in asthma exacerbations in adults suggests that children, upon returning to school, are sharing colds and cold viruses that they bring to school after summer vacation, causing a rise in colds and a rise in asthma exacerbations. These colds are then brought home and affect parents with asthma.

Other Considerations About Asthma During School Return

The return to school is a time when many kids go back to participating in organized sports. For kids with asthma, it is an important time to be prepared. Many children have asthma brought on by exercise, and September and October are peak seasons for ragweed pollen in many areas of the United States. As school-age children (and college students) get back to the routine of regular exercise, they must be taking their controller medications regularly, if directed by their asthma care provider.

Asthmatics with symptoms brought on by exercise can often minimize their symptoms with premedication, taking two puffs of albuterol fifteen to thirty minutes before strenuous exercise.

Younger children may need to have their parents work with the school nurse so that asthma medications are readily available in case quick relief is needed. Ask your asthma care provider to provide an extra prescription for quick-relief medication to be kept with the school nurse or health office so that it is available if a child runs out or forgets to keep it handy. For children who have severe allergies to foods or bees, an EpiPen should be kept with the school nurse in case of a reaction.

Schools all have different policies about keeping medications and different systems to care for kids when they are sick in school. Parents should check with their child's school to become familiar with what they have in place and how they can work with them to keep their child's asthma under the best control in school as they do at home.

MANAGING ASTHMA IN THE SCHOOL ENVIRONMENT

Many indoor air quality problems in schools can impact the health of students and staff, including those with asthma. Some of the indoor air quality problems include: chemical pollutants from building or building maintenance materials; chemical pollutants from science and art classes; improperly maintained ventilation systems; and allergens from classroom animals and cockroaches or pests.

Mold growth may result from standing water in maintenance rooms, or excess moisture in ceiling tiles, carpets, and other furnishings. Also, outdoor air pollutants and pollens may enter the school through ventilation systems and/or open doors and windows.

Control Animal Allergens

Classes may commonly adopt animals as a classroom pet or science project. School staff may not realize that any warm-blooded animals, including gerbils, birds, cats, dogs, mice, and rats, may trigger asthma. Proteins that act as allergens in the dander, urine, or saliva of warm-blooded animals may sensitize individuals and cause allergic reactions or trigger asthma episodes in people sensitive to animal allergens.

Common Sources Found In School Settings

The most common, obvious source of the animal allergen is having a pet in the classroom or school. If an animal is present in the school, there is a possibility of direct, daily exposure to the animal's dander and bodily fluids. It is important to realize that, even after extensive cleaning, pet allergen levels may stay in the indoor environment several months after the animal is removed.

The most effective method of controlling exposure to animal allergens in schools is to keep your school free of feathered or furred animals. However, for some individuals, isolation measures may be sufficiently effective. Isolation measures include: keeping animals in localized areas, keeping animals away from upholstered furniture, carpets, and stuffed toys, and keeping sensitive individuals away from animals as much as possible.

For schools with animals, it is important to make sure that classrooms containing animals are frequently and thoroughly cleaned. In addition, animal allergens can readily migrate to other areas of the school environment through the air and children who handle pets. Therefore, the entire building should be cleaned thoroughly.

Schools are sometimes advised to use air cleaners. Although properly used and maintained air cleaners may be effective for reducing animal dander in small areas, they should only be considered as an addition to other control methods. It is also important to carefully review information on the type of air cleaner used to make sure it is suitably sized and has high particle removal efficiency. In addition, some air-cleaning devices marketed as air purifiers emit ozone, which may be harmful to people with asthma.

Suggestions For Reducing Exposures In Schools

Remove animals from the school, if possible. If completely removing animals from the school is not possible, then try the following:

- Keep animals in cages or localized areas as much as possible; do not let them roam.

- Clean cages regularly. Consider using disposable gloves when cleaning.
- Locate animals away from ventilation system (vents) to avoid circulating allergens throughout the room or building.
- Locate sensitive students as far away from animals and their habitats as possible.
- Keep animals away from upholstered furniture, carpets, and stuffed toys.

Clean Up Mold And Control Moisture

Molds can be found almost anywhere, and they can grow on virtually any substance, where moisture is present. Outdoors, many molds live in the soil and play a key role in breaking leaves, wood, and other plant debris. Without molds, we would be struggling with large amounts of dead plant matter.

Molds produce tiny spores which reproduce. Mold spores travel through the indoor and outdoor air continually. When mold spores land on a damp spot indoors, they may begin growing and digesting whatever they are growing on to survive. Some molds can grow on wood, paper, carpet, and foods. If excessive moisture or water accumulates indoors, extensive mold growth may occur, particularly if the moisture problem remains undiscovered or unaddressed. There is no practical way to eliminate all mold and mold spores in the indoor environment—the way to control indoor mold growth is to control moisture. If mold is a problem in your school, you must clean up the mold and eliminate sources of moisture.

Common Moisture Sources Found In Schools.

Various conditions can cause moisture problems in school buildings, including roof and plumbing leaks, condensation, and excess humidity. Some moisture problems in schools have been linked to changes in building construction practices during the past twenty to thirty years. These changes have resulted in more tightly sealed buildings that may not allow moisture to escape easily. Moisture problems in schools are also associated with delayed maintenance or insufficient maintenance due to budget and other constraints.

Temporary structures in schools, such as trailers and portable classrooms, have frequently been associated with moisture and mold problems.

Suggestions For Reducing Mold Growth In Schools

Reduce indoor humidity using the following methods:

- Vent showers and other moisture-generating sources to the outside.
- Control humidity levels and dampness by using air conditioners and de-humidifiers
- Provide adequate ventilation to maintain indoor humidity levels between thirty–sixty percent.
- Use exhaust fans whenever cooking, dishwashing, and cleaning in food service areas. Inspect buildings for signs of mold, moisture, leaks, or spills.
- Check for moldy odors.
- Look for water stains or discoloration on the ceilings, walls, floors, and window sills.
- Look around and under sinks for standing water, water stains, or mold.
- Inspect bathrooms for standing water, water stains, or mold.
- Do not let water stand in air conditioning or refrigerator drip pans.

Respond promptly when you see signs of moisture and/or mold or when leaks or spills occur:

- Clean and dry any damp or wet building materials and furnishings within twenty-four–forty-eight hours of occurrence to prevent mold growth.

- Repair the source of the water problem or leak to prevent mold growth.
- Clean mold off hard surfaces with water and detergent, and dry completely.
- Replace absorbent materials such as ceiling tiles that are moldy.
- Check the mechanical room and roof for unsanitary conditions, leaks, or spills.

Prevent moisture condensation using the following methods:

- Reduce the potential for condensation on cold surfaces (e.g., windows, piping, exterior walls, roof, or floors) by adding insulation.
- For floor and carpet cleaning, remove spots and stains immediately, using the flooring manufacturer's recommended techniques. Use care to prevent excess moisture or cleaning residue accumulation and ensure that cleaned areas are dried quickly.
- Do not install carpeting in areas where there is a perpetual moisture problem, (e.g., by drinking fountains, by classroom sinks, or on concrete floors with leaks or frequent condensation).

Control Cockroach And Pest Allergens

Cockroach allergens may play a significant role in asthma throughout inner-city, suburban, and rural schools. Certain proteins which act as allergens in the waste products and saliva of cockroaches can cause allergic reactions or trigger asthma symptoms in some individuals.

Pest allergens are a significant cause of occupational asthma symptoms among laboratory workers, such as scientists who work with animals in scientific investigations. These allergens may also contribute to allergies and asthma in the general population.

Common Sources Found In School Settings

Cockroaches and other pests, such as rats and mice, are often found in the school setting. Allergens from these pests may be significant asthma triggers for students and staff in schools. Pest problems in schools may be caused or worsened by various conditions such as plumbing leaks, moisture problems, and improper food handling and storage practices. In order to manage a pest problem, water and food sources need to be controlled in the school environment. Therefore, it is important to avoid exposure to these allergens through the use of common sense, Integrated Pest Management (IPM) practices throughout the entire school.

There are four key IPM methods for reducing exposure to pests in the school setting:

- Look for signs of pests.
- Do not leave food, water, or garbage exposed.
- Remove pest pathways and shelters.
- Use pest control products such as poison baits, traps, and pesticide sprays, as needed.

Eliminate Secondhand Smoke Exposure

Secondhand smoke is the smoke from the burning end of a cigarette, pipe, or cigar and the smoke breathed out by a smoker. Secondhand smoke exposure causes several serious health effects in young children, such as coughing and wheezing, bronchitis and pneumonia, ear infections, reduced lung function and increased asthma attacks. Secondhand smoke is an irritant that may trigger an asthma episode, and increasing evidence suggests secondhand smoke may cause asthma in children.

The Environmental Protection Agency estimates that between two hundred thousand and one million children with asthma have their condition made worse by exposure to secondhand smoke. Secondhand smoke can also lead to the buildup of fluid in the middle ear, the most common cause of children being hospitalized for an operation.

Common Sources Found In School Settings

The majority of schools in the United States prohibit smoking on school grounds. However, constantly smoking occurs in school bathrooms, lounges, and on school grounds. This may cause problems for students and staff who have asthma. It is important to enforce smoking bans on school grounds to prevent exposure to secondhand smoke. If smoking occurs within the building, secondhand smoke can travel through the ventilation system to the entire school. Also, even when people smoke outside, secondhand smoke may enter the school through the ventilation system, open windows, and doors.

To reduce secondhand smoke exposure in schools, smoking bans must be enforced on school property.

Reduce Exposure To Dust Mites

Dust mite allergens play a significant role in asthma. These allergens may cause an allergic reaction or trigger an asthma episode in sensitive individuals. In addition, there is evidence that dust mites cause new cases of asthma in susceptible children.

Dust mites are too small to be seen but are found in homes, schools, and other buildings throughout the United States. Dust mites live in mattresses, pillows, carpets, fabric-covered furniture, bedcovers, clothes, and stuffed toys.

Common Sources Found In Schools

Dust mites may be found in schools in carpeting, upholstered furniture, stuffed animals or toys, and pillows. Stuffed animals or toys, as well as pillows for taking naps, are used mostly in the primary grades. Suggestions for reducing exposure to dust mites in schools include the following:

- Choose washable stuffed toys and wash them often in hot water.
- Cover pillows in dust-proof (allergen-impermeable), zipped covers.
- Remove dust from hard surfaces, often with a damp cloth, vacuum carpeting, and fabric-covered furniture to reduce dust buildup. Allergic people should leave the area being vacuumed. Vacuums with high efficiency filters (HEPA) or central vacuums may be helpful.

TRAVELING WITH ASTHMA

The fun of traveling is going to a completely different place. But if you have asthma, a new environment can seem less fun because there's always the worry that something unexpected may cause an asthma attack. But you can take steps to help avoid problems while you're away from home—so you can concentrate on the fun.

Before You Go

Before you leave, make sure your asthma is well controlled. If it has been flaring up, check with your doctor before you head off on your trip. He or she may need to adjust your medicine or ask you to come in for a visit.

When packing, remember all the medicine you are taking for your asthma, including relief and controller medicines. Keep your medications in your carry-on bags, so they're always with you. It's also a good idea to pack a little extra medication so you don't run out while you're on the road. If you are leaving the country, it can help to have a letter from your doctor that describes your asthma and your medicines. This can help you with airport security or customs. You also might want to know the generic names of your medicines. These are the chemical names of the medicine, not the brand name the drug company has given it. If you need to get a refill in another country, the medication might have a different brand name. You can get the generic names from your doctor's office or pharmacist.

Other things to pack include your peak flow meter (if you use one), a copy of your asthma action plan, your health insurance card, and your doctor's phone number.

Windows Up Or Down?

Trains, buses, and even your family car might have dust mites and mold trapped in the upholstery or the ventilation system. You can't do much about a bus or train (except make sure you've taken your controller medication and have your rescue medication handy). But if you're traveling by car, ask the driver to run the air conditioner or heater with the windows open for at least ten minutes. If pollen or air pollution triggers your asthma and counts are high during your trip, travel with the windows closed and the air conditioner on.

Finding The Friendly Skies

All flights within the United States are smoke-free, but some international flights are not. If you find yourself on one of these flights, ask to be seated as far from the smoking section as possible. The air on planes is also very dry, and this can trigger an asthma attack. Make sure you have your rescue medications handy, and try to drink a lot of water.

Home Away From Home

If you're staying in a hotel, you may find that something in the room triggers your asthma. Requesting a sunny, dry room away from the hotel's pool might help. If animal allergens trigger your asthma, ask for a room that has never had pets in it. And you should always stay in a nonsmoking room, bringing your blanket and pillow can also help prevent a flare-up.

If you're staying with family or friends, tell them in advance about your triggers. They won't be able to clear away all dust mites or mold, but they can dust and vacuum carefully, especially in the room you'll sleep in. You also can ask them to avoid using scented candles, potpourri, or aerosol products, if those bother you.

Just like at home, you'll want to avoid tobacco smoke. Ask anyone who smokes to step outside, especially if you're sharing a room. Wood fires in the fireplace or woodstove also could be a problem for you.

Traveling On Your Own

If possible, carry a copy of your asthma action plan so people who are traveling with you (or the people you're staying with) can help if you have any breathing trouble. If you don't have a copy of your plan, let these people know which medicines you take, what the dosages are, and the number where your parents and your doctor can be reached in case of an emergency.

Without your parents along you will have more responsibility for your asthma. Keep your triggers in mind and take steps to avoid them. If pollen bothers you, find out what the readings are on a day when you'll be going for a hike or taking part in other outdoor activities. If air pollution bothers you, make sure you keep that in mind when you're visiting a smoggy city. Cities like Los Angeles make information on air pollution levels available through their weather services.

If you're planning to participate in any new activities while you're away, talk to your doctor about them before you leave. And whatever you do, make sure your relief medication is nearby in case you need it.

Of course, you'll want to forget about your asthma and have fun while you're away. And the best way to do this is by planning and having your medication with you—so you don't have to worry if you do have a flareup. If you ignore your asthma completely by not taking precautions, there's chance you could end up in the emergency department. And that's no way to spend a vacation.

METERED DOSE INHALER & HAND HELD NEBULIZER

Inhaled respiratory medications are often taken by using a device called a metered dose inhaler, or MDI. The MDI is a pressurized canister of medicine in a plastic holder with a mouthpiece. When sprayed, it gives a reliable, consistent dose of medication.

There are two methods for using an MDI. In many cases, the preferred method is with a device called a valved holding chamber or spacer. These devices attach to the MDI and hold the "spray" of medication. They make it easier to use the MDI and help get the medication into the lungs better. An MDI can also be used without a spacer. These methods are described below. Your doctor will decide which method is most appropriate for you.

Priming: Priming (spraying one or more puffs into the air before use) assures that the inhaler is ready to use and will dispense the correct amount of medication. Priming varies between devices, so it is important to read the patient instructions that come with your medication. I learned about Priming from my allergist, Dr. James Thompson. When I began using Proair MDI, it requires priming.

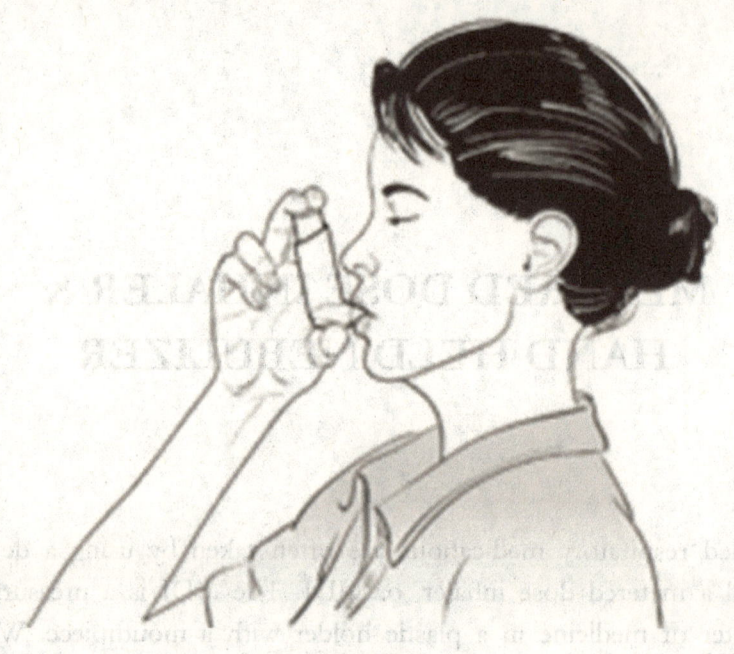

Figure 1

Using an MDI without a chamber (Figure 1)
1. Remove the cap from the MDI and shake well.
2. Breathe out all the way.
3. Place the mouthpiece of the inhaler between your teeth and seal your lips tightly around it.
4. As you start to breathe in slowly, press down on the canister one time.
5. Keep breathing in as slowly and as deeply as you can. (It should take about 5 seconds for you to completely breathe in.)
6. Hold your breath for ten seconds (count to ten slowly) to allow the medication to reach the airways of the lungs.
7. Repeat the above steps for each puff ordered by your doctor. Wait about 1 minute between puffs.

8. Replace the cap on the MDI when finished.

9. Use a valved holding chamber as described below if you are using a corticosteroid MDI.

Using an MDI with a valved holding chamber (Figure 2)

1. Remove the cap from the MDI and chamber. Shake well.

2. Insert the MDI into the open end of the chamber (opposite the mouthpiece).

3. Place the mouthpiece of the chamber between your teeth and seal your lips tightly around it.

4. Breathe out completely.

5. Press the canister once.

6. Breathe in slowly and completely through your mouth. If you hear a "horn-like" sound, you are breathing too quickly and need to slow down.

7. Hold your breath for ten seconds (count to ten slowly) to allow the medication to reach the airways of the lung.

8. Repeat the above steps for each puff ordered by your doctor. Wait about 1 minute in between puffs.

9. Replace the cap on your MDI when finished.

10. Rinse your mouth and gargle using water or mouthwash after each use if you are using a corticosteroid MDI (i.e. serevent, flovent). This is very important because you can develop oral thrush. Oral thrush is an infection where fungus accumulates in the mouth. It appears as white spots on the tongue or on the back of the throat. You should always use a chamber with a steroid MDI.

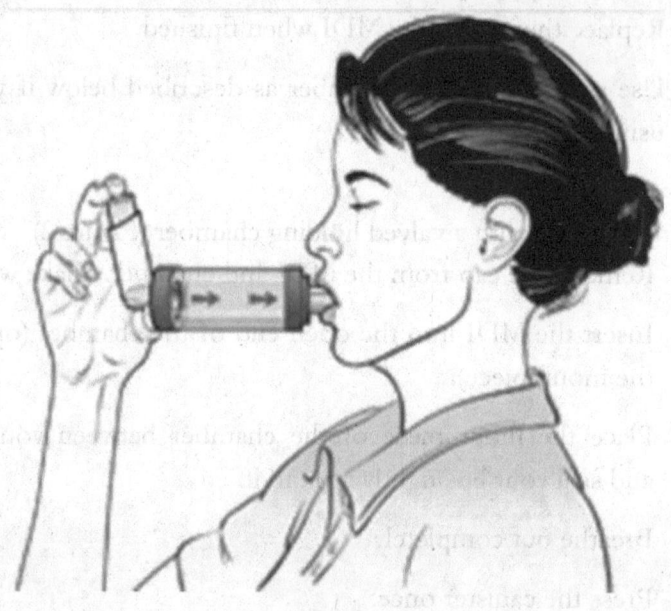

Figure 2

A nebulizer is a piece of medical equipment that a person with asthma or another respiratory condition can use to administer the medication directly and quickly to the lungs.

A nebulizer turns liquid medicine into a very fine mist that a person can inhale through a face mask or mouth piece. Taking medicine this way allows it to go directly into the lungs where it is needed.

Who needs a nebulizer?

Doctors typically prescribe nebulizers to people with one of the following lung disorders: Asthma, Chronic Obstructive Pulmonary Disease (COPD), Cystic Fibrosis, Bronchiectasis, and Bronchiolitius. Before a person starts taking medicine with a nebulizer, a doctor, respiratory therapist, or nurse will explain how the nebulizer works and answer any questions.

If a person receives their nebulizer from a pharmacy or medical equipment company, someone will explain how to use it.

Each nebulizing machine operates a little differently. It is crucial to read the instructions for the particular device that the doctor has prescribed.

In general, a nebulizer is very easy to use, with only a few basic steps:

- Wash your hands.
- Add the medicine to the medicine cup, according to the doctor's prescription.
- Assemble the top piece, tubing, mask, or mouth piece.
- Attach the tubing to the machine according to the instructions. Turn the nebulizer on; they can be battery- or electrically powered.
- While using the nebulizer, hold the mouthpiece and medicine cup upright to help deliver all the medication.
- Take slow, deep breaths through the mouthpiece until all the medicine is used. Please speak with the doctor or call the manufacturer with any questions or concerns about the device.

Is a prescription necessary?

A nebulizer and the medicine it uses requires a prescription from a doctor.

It is possible to purchase a nebulizer machine online without a prescription, though a doctor will still need to prescribe the medication.

However, some medication manufacturers require the use of a specific type of nebulizer, so it is always a good idea to double-check with the pharmacist or doctor before making a purchase.

There are several types of medication that a person can use with a nebulizer:

Bronchodilators: These are drugs that help open the airways and make breathing easier. Doctors often prescribe bronchodilators to people with asthma, COPD, or other respiratory disorders.

Sterile saline solution: A nebulizer can deliver sterile saline to help open the airways and thin secretions. This may loosen and make it easier to cough up mucus in the lungs.

Antibiotics: A nebulizer can deliver some types of antibiotics straight into the lungs or respiratory tract when someone has a severe respiratory infection.

Differences between nebulizers and inhalers

Nebulizers and inhalers have some similarities — for example, they deliver medicine directly into the lungs to help make breathing easier. However, there are some important differences.

There are two types of inhalers: a metered-dose inhaler (MDI) and a dry-powder inhaler.

An MDI is the most common type of inhaler. Using one involves inhaling a pre measured amount of medicine through a mouth piece. Some inhalers have a spacer, which makes it easier to inhale the medication.

A dry-powder inhaler is similar, but the medication is in powder form inside the inhaler. It requires the user to take a deep, fast breath, which pulls the powdered medicine deep into the lungs.

Both types require the ability to inhale the medicine deep within the lungs. Some children and people with severe respiratory diseases may find this problematic.

Nebulizers tend to be a little easier to use in terms of delivering the medicine. However, a nebulizer may take up to ten minutes to dispense the medication, and the user needs to sit still until they have inhaled all of it, which may be hard for a young child.

Also, some nebulizers are not as portable as others; they can be difficult to carry around, while inhalers are typically smaller and more suitable for traveling.

HOW TO MAINTAIN A NEBULIZER

The Respiratory Therapist or pharmacist will demonstrate how to clean and maintain the device. The general guidelines are as follows:

- Wash your hands and work on a clean surface.

- Disconnect the tube, medicine chamber, mask, or mouthpiece, and wash them thoroughly in warm, soapy water. Rinse then, soak in disinfection solution (white vinegar and water) Rinse again.

- Allow the pieces to air dry on a clean towel.

- Disinfect the machine according to the manufacturer's instructions.

- Replace some component pieces between three and four times per year. Consult the instruction manual to learn how and how often to do this. Also, make sure never to share pieces with another person.

- Follow the instructions for cleaning, disinfecting, and replacement.

- Take good care of a nebulizer or it can become contaminated with bacteria that can cause a dangerous infection.

WHERE SHOULD A NEBULIZER BE USED?

Use the nebulizer in a well-lighted area. Select a comfortable place in your home where you can take your treatment without being interrupted. Sit in a comfortable, straight-backed chair when taking your treatment.

Treatment procedure

1. Place the compressor on a sturdy surface that will support its weight, such as a table or desk. Plug the compressor's cord into a properly grounded (three-pronged) outlet.

2. Wash your hands with soap and water and dry completely with a clean towel.

3. Become familiar with the nebulizer parts.

4. Place your medication in the nebulizer cup.

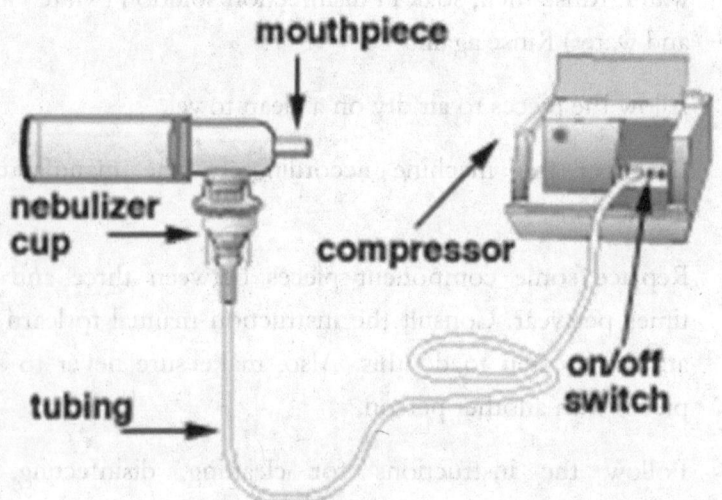

5. Attach the top portion of the nebulizer cup, and connect the mouthpiece or face mask to the cup.

6. Connect the tubing to the nebulizer and compressor.

7. Turn on the compressor with the on/off switch. Once you turn on the compressor, you should see a light mist.

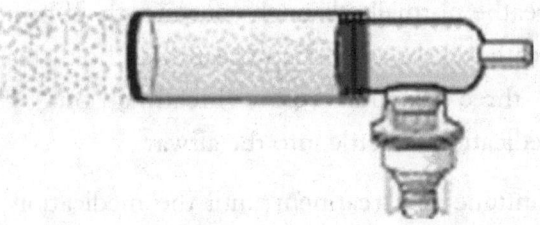

8. Sit up straight on a comfortable chair.

9. Use a mouthpiece, which is preferred. When using a mouthpiece, place the mouthpiece between your teeth and seal your lips around it.

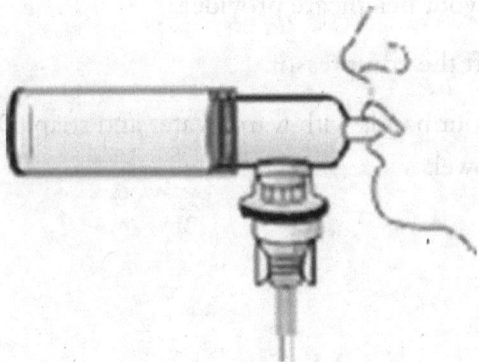

If you are using a mask, position it comfortably and securely on your face.

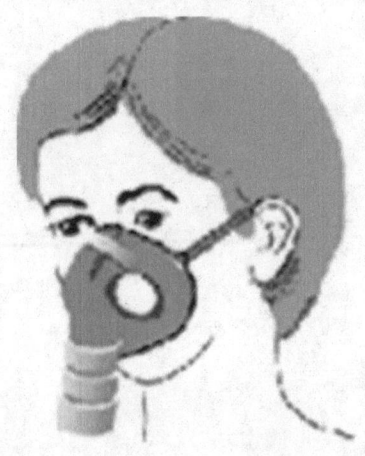

1. Breathe normally through your mouth. If possible, every fifth breath, take a slow deep breath and hold this breath for two to three seconds before breathing out. This allows the medication to settle into the airways.

2. Continue the treatment until the medication is gone (about five to fifteen minutes). Use all of the medicine unless you are directed otherwise by your doctor.

3. Slow your breathing or rest briefly if you become dizzy. Some medicine may make you feel "jittery" or "shaky." This is not uncommon, but if these symptoms continue to bother you, inform your healthcare provider.

4. Turn off the compressor.

5. Wash your hands with warm water and soap. Dry them with a clean towel.

BEST PRACTICES FOR EATING OUT

I know when I was a kid I loved going out to dinner at sit-down restaurants. My parents required that we knew proper etiquette at the dinner table before we were allowed to dine in restaurants. In order to safely dine in restaurants or even fast food here are a few tips that I have found helpful.

1. Check the menu. Most menus can be found online or using restaurant apps on your mobile device. If you have questions, call and ask for clarification.

2. Let everyone in your party know you have food allergies. If someone orders something you are allergic to, be sure there is no cross-contamination with the bread basket or any other shared trays or baskets on the table.

3. Let the wait staff know you have food allergies if you know that your allergens are on the menu.

4. Do not share food or eat out of any plate but your own.

DR. RENEE'S RESTAURANTS

STEAK
1. Wildfire – Chicago, IL
2. Smith & Wollensky – Chicago, IL

BRUNCH
3. Sweet Maple Café – Chicago, IL
4. Batter and Berries – Chicago, IL
5. The Breakfast Club – Commerce Twp., MI
6. IHOP
7. Flying Biscuit – Atlanta, GA
8. Ruby Slipper – New Orleans, LA

BAKERY
9. City Cakes Bakery - NYC

PIZZA
10. Jets Pizza
11. Little Caesars Pizza
12. Domino's Pizza
13. Lou Malnati's Pizza – Chicago, IL

FRANCHISES

1. Red Lobster

2. Boston Market

3. KFC

4. Church's Chicken

5. Popeyes Chicken

6. McDonald's

7. Wendy's

8. Burger King

9. White Castle

10. Panera Bread

11. Cosi

12. Chipotle

13. TGI Friday's

14. Olive Garden

15. Red Robin

COMMON ALLERGENS

1. Cow's Milk
2. Eggs
3. Tree Nuts
4. Peanuts
5. Shellfish
6. Wheat
7. Soy
8. Fish
9. Raw Fruits and Vegetables
10. Sesame Seeds
11. Mold/Mildew
12. Dust
13. Ragweed
14. Pollen
15. Pet Dander

ABOUT THE AUTHOR

Dr. Reneé Matthews is a leader in the healthcare industry. She has spent the early part of her career as a medical educator and a radio host for a satellite show.

Dr. Matthews was awarded the 2013 Friend of Mobile CARE Award for her commitment to raising awareness of asthma in her current city of Chicago. In addition to writing about health, she conducts speaking engagements on social media, motivation, and inspiration and provides business advice to start-ups and entrepreneurs.

She has been featured in Ebony and Essence magazines. Dr. Matthews was a contributing writer for *Good Enough Mother*, *Essence*, *MadameNoire*, and *Black and Married with Kids*, where she reported health news and health care. Along with her columns, Dr. Matthews has often appeared as a lecturer before various organizations nationwide.

She's drawn from her experiences while putting her expertise to work for several media outlets and the talk show circuit. As a long-time asthmatic, she has become a passionate advocate for asthma education. She addresses the concerns asthma sufferers have to get their best possible health and medical care by supplying them with tools and knowledge they need to navigate the healthcare system, stay safe in the pursuit of care, and engaging patients to be active participants in their health and healthcare. Most recently, she has appeared on her show "Out of Office with Dr. Renee," which is seen in more than 45,000 doctors' offices across the country.

Dr. Matthews is an active member of the Girl Scouts and a mentor to Save a Girl Save a World. She is incredibly passionate about addressing the health concerns of Black women and has been recognized by patients and professionals alike for her ability to translate the challenges patients face into tools and solutions they can use to improve their health care.

ACKNOWLEDGMENTS

God, the person behind everything, made sure I was born with the right parents to handle all my medical emergencies. My mom, I have always wanted to be just like her because she is the smartest woman I know. I am just the wild version of her. My Padre showed me entrepreneurship firsthand and gave me this excellent West Indian blood more specifically Ladoo bloodline that has contributed to who I am and capable of doing.

My sissy is my biggest support because no matter what I say I want to do, she believes I can do it even when I have no faith. Eva Wilson aka Socamom, I can only thank GOD that we met years ago and then reconnected a few years ago. Our weekly teatime has been so beneficial to both of us in creating content to help our communities to flourish. You helped me outline this book, gave me my title, designed my book cover. I appreciate you more than you will ever know. Dr. Kelly Wood, I would have never made it thru 2020 without you. Thank you for your listening ear and your prayers. You told me I could write this book and wouldn't let me turn back once I started the ball rolling. Selam, my BFF, you, and Alycia are the head of my front office and continue to remind me that if anyone can do it, I can. Cassandra Cummings, my coach, thank you for your great mastermind, which was just the fire I needed to get this project done once and for all. Draka, my money coach, who left me alone so that I could finish this book. Now, Draka, we can get back to winning in the market. Brandi Riley, my coach, has helped me get this book to all the right places and people and allowed me to have all the conversations I needed to have with the media and press about it.

Dr. James Thompson, my allergist, who helped me through different thoughts while writing this book. Dr. Margena A. Christian, without your help during the editing and the publishing process, this would not have been a notion. Dr. Rachael Ross, my friend and mentor, who showed me firsthand that doctors don't have to only see patients; we can do many other things. Thank you to Jeannee Turner. I met you when I was a camper at OCC camp and all these years later you are still there for me. Thank you for helping me with this book.

Finally, to Kim and Janeille, who regularly encourage me to go after my dreams and do things that make me scared and uncomfortable. They are the greatest sounding board ever for thoughts and ideas.

REFERENCES

WEBSITES

MEDICALNEWS
www.medicalnews.com

ASTHMA AND ALLERGY FOUNDATION OF AMERICA
www.aafa.org

FOOD AWARENESS
www.foodalleryawareness.org

ALLERGY AND ASTHMA NETWORK, MOTHERS OF ASTHMATIC
www.aabma.org

ASTHMA INITIATIVE OF MICHIGAN
www.getasthmahelp.org

GLOBAL INITIATIVE
www.ginasthma.org

CLEVELAND CLINIC
my.clevelandclinic.org

OTHER SOURCES

Asthma overview. American Academy of Allergy Asthma and Immunology.
www.aaaai.org/conditions-and treatments/asthma.aspx
Cambridge S, Cambridge TC. Asthma in adolescents and adults.

Fanta CH. Treatment of acute exacerbation of asthma in adults. Last updated,

www.uptodate.com/contents/treatment-of-acute-exacerbations-of-asthma-in-adults

Global Initiative for Asthma. Pocket Guide for Asthma Management and Prevention (for Adults and Children Older than 5 Years). Johnson J. Asthma assessment tips. *J Nurse Pract.* 2010;6(5):383-4.

Kaufman G. Asthma: pathophysiology, diagnosis and management. *Nursing Standard*

Martinez FD, Vercelli D. Asthma. *Lancet Sem.*

National Asthma Education and Prevention

Program. Expert Panel Report 3: Guidelines for the Diagnosis and Management of Asthma.

Section 2: Definition, pathophysiology and pathogenesis of asthma and natural history of asthma. Bethesda, MD: National Heart, Lung, and Blood Institute; 2007; 1-24.

Pruitt B, Lawson R. Assessing and managing asthma: a Global Initiative for Asthma update.

Nursing. 2011; 41(5):46-52.

INDEX

allergens, 12, 35, 45, 63, 83, 91, 100, 101, 109, 112, 120, 136, 139, 142, 146, 163, 165, 167, 168, 171, 172, 198, 199, 202, 203, 219

anaphylaxis, 35, 160, 161

asthma, 1, 2, 3, 5, 7, 8, 9, 11, 12, 13, 14, 15, 17, 20, 22, 23, 24, 26, 27, 31, 32, 35, 37, 38, 41, 42, 43, 50, 53, 66, 68, 72, 77, 78, 79, 82, 83, 84, 85, 86, 89, 90, 91, 92, 94, 95, 96, 97, 100, 101, 102, 103, 104, 107, 108, 109, 110, 111, 113, 114, 115, 116,118, 119, 120, 121, 122, 123, 124, 125, 129, 130, 132, 136, 138, 140, 141, 142, 143, 144, 145, 146, 147, 149, 150, 151, 152, 153, 154, 155, 156, 157, 166, 170, 171, 172, 175, 176, 182, 183, 184, 185, 186, 187, 188, 189, 191, 192, 194, 195, 196, 198, 202, 203, 204, 206, 207, 208, 212, 223, 227, 228

Asthma, 81, 97, 176

Asthma Action Plan, 38

asthma attack, 1, 7, 9, 12, 13, 23, 24, 26, 53, 82, 84, 86, 90, 102, 146, 147, 149, 151, 206, 207

breathing treatment, 48

Chobani, 36

cockroaches, 134, 146, 193, 202

corticosteroids, 144

Dust mites, 112

eczema, 110, 123, 137, 161, 170, 171, 172, 173

environment, 35, 137

Epinephrine, 45, 58, 167

EpiPen, 44, 55

gastrointestinal, 51

mold, 33, 91, 109, 110, 162, 167, 200, 201

mold spores, 200

nebulizer, 35, 37, 212, 213, 214, 215, 216

Oatly, 36
peak flow meter, 38, 86, 87, 207
pet dander, 167
Prednisone, 37, 153
Pulmonary Function Test, 66
pulmonologist, 8, 67
Scratch Skin Test, 164
triggers, 2, 8, 19, 23, 83, 85, 101, 119, 139, 142, 144, 146, 153, 156, 171, 172, 182, 186, 190, 192, 207

www.ingramcontent.com/pod-product-compliance
Lightning Source LLC
Chambersburg PA
CBHW050045120526